CHASING TIGERS IN THE DARK

Life Lessons of a *Fierce* Survivor

ALLY SHAW

LIBRARY TALES PUBLISHING
www.LibraryTalesPublishing.com
www.Facebook.com/LibraryTalesPublishing

For general information on our other products and services, please contact our Customer Care Department at 1-800-754-5016, or fax 917-463-0892. For technical support, please visit www.LibraryTalesPublishing.com

Library Tales Publishing also publishes its books in a variety of electronic formats. Every content that appears in print is available in electronic books.

978-1-736241-88-2
978-1-956769-07-4

PRINTED IN THE UNITED STATES OF AMERICA

CONTENTS

BIO

Ally Shaw is a born and bred Virginian. She has a deep love for animals, music, and traveling. Ally is an enthusiastic foodie, and even more so loves bougie coffee and French champagne. She is a fierce survivor who has reinvented herself multiple times after devastating loss. Ally is a cancer survivor who became an opera singer. Ally is a divorced single mom of two who found the love of her life, married, and became a mom to a blended family of seven amazing children at age thirty-six. Ally is an entrepreneur, core value ambassador, and is deeply passionate about helping others to become their best selves, especially after trauma. Ally earned a bachelor's degree from Elon University and a master's degree from Loyola University New Orleans. Ally and her husband own a seventeen location multi-unit Domino's Pizza franchise in Virginia and West Virginia, are six time Gold Franny winners (top 2% of Domino's franchisees world wide) and employ over 300 people. Ally and her husband are passionate about giving back to kids and families in need and have financially supported St. Jude Children's Hospital for decades. Ally is a first-time author of the book "Chasing Tigers in the Dark, Life Lessons of a Fierce Survivor" and launched a new career as a motivational speaker at age forty. Ally splits her time between Blacksburg, Virginia and Sunset Beach, North Carolina where you can find her searching for sand dollars with her dogs Maggie and Moët.

Disclaimer:

The events, places and conversations in this book have been recreated from memory. The chronology of some events has been slightly condensed in some cases. The names and identifying characteristics of a few individuals have been changed to maintain anonymity. The author and publisher have no liability or responsibility to any person or entity with respect to any potential loss or damage caused by the information contained in this book.

Dedication
To all three of my parents...

To David & Libby who gave me life and then saved it multiple times. Without your love and support I would have a very different life or no life at all. I love you both so much and appreciate all you do!

To the strongest woman I have ever known, Bette. I cannot imagine living a life that you are not a part of, and I continue to mourn your passing every single day. I love you more than you will ever know and hope this book will allow your legacy to live on for decades to come.

INTRODUCTION

Hey friend! Thank you for buying my book and embarking on a journey toward abundant mental health wellness with me. I chose the book title, "Chasing Tigers in the Dark" because I cannot imagine anything braver. I also believe sometimes the things we cannot see scare us the most and living in the darkness of our past prevents us from living a deeply passionate life. I have been thinking about hashtags a lot lately too. Hashtags are all around us and exist on every social media platform. Sometimes they are symbolic of a political, cultural, or social justice movement. Sometimes the hashtags are more personal. My dominant hashtag at this moment (#stayfierce) is a directive on how I intend to live my life after two decades of stumbling through the dark. The second part of the book title, "Life Lessons of a Fierce Survivor" provides a couple of clues about what I will cover in this book but for now, allow me to encourage you to #stayfierce as you begin the process of conquering your own demons. The phrase #stayfierce represents equal parts passion and bravery, and this is the dynamic duo that allowed me to move forward after trauma. It is time, dear friend, to boldly resurface from the black abyss, guided by the light of hope as a survivor.

I am a proud survivor, having endured some of the worst traumas a person can face including the loss of a parent, a serious personal battle with an aggressive cancer, a brutal sodomized rape, the horrific death of my first love, a complicated divorce, a couple of near-death accidents, chronic health issues, ten surgeries, and an incestuous sexual assault. This book is my gift to people who are struggling to heal from trauma and provides valuable life lessons for the nightmares we attempt to choke down to the deepest depths of our consciousness. Writing this book began as a therapeutic exercise and by the time I finished it, I had found freedom and forgiveness from the horrific events that plagued my past and distracted me from a promising future. Much of my trauma occurred in my twenties; however, my inability to work through it allowed it to continue to dramatically affect me into my thirties and forties. I crafted the adjective "traumaniacal" as I feel it depicts the complete picture of who I became from my unresolved chronic traumatic experiences. In other words, I was not just a person living with general anxiety. My particular anxiety composition was a paint by numbers situation with layers of pigments and binders. The palette of colors was divergent and the scene confusing as it obeyed no rules. The paint was thick and permanent. I lived dormant in that once sticky, now hardened place for two decades, which made my mental health condition require a more complicated definition.

Definition: Traumaniacal
Crafted by Ally Shaw
Traumaniacal (adjective)1 :exceeding traditional anxiety markers. Often caused by
unresolved, chronic trauma in various categories to include loss, illness, abuse, rape.

You are about to read the story of a traumaniacal mess who
became a trauma miracle. If you choose to read my book, I
hope you too will wake up refreshed with hope and primed
for action to create the happy life you are so deserving of. It
only takes a moment to make the decision to live a totally
different life, free from the constraints of the evil that attempted to destroy you. Before you read further, I do want
to be clear about something. This book is not intended to be
a religious book; although it does pander in various genres,
including self-help, women's empowerment, personal devel-
opment, and spiritual enlightenment. I wade carefully into
the Christian inspiration category and talk about my faith
as it is relevant to the story. It is important to me, however;
that I share my deeply founded belief that the choice to be
in a relationship with God (or not to be) is a very personal
decision. I am trying very hard to simply share my story
of recovery and not come across as preachy. I have been
burned, as many of you likely have, by religious leaders and
organizations that claimed to be one thing and after careful
examination, ended up being quite the opposite. My number one goal is to help as many people with my story as
possible, no matter what your beliefs, background or experiences entail. I hope you will read on with an open mind
and heart and I pray that my words will bring you comfort
and hope. I believe in you, my new friend. Now, how about
we dive right in and talk tigers!?!

My first encounter with a baby tiger occurred in North
Carolina at a local ranch. The ranch, which was really a zoo's
little sister, was owned by a man who passionately cared
for and trained tigers. It was a grassroots operation, but the

charming venue drew me in immediately and had massive potential to be so much more. My husband and I pulled into the dusty dirt parking lot, unloaded the double stroller from the Chevy Trailblazer, and unbuckled two excited toddlers. My parents trailed two car lengths behind us and found a parking space closer to the entrance. The ranch was open to the public; however, the organic home-grown character of the property was captivating. The owner greeted us when we walked in and I immediately felt like family. The ranch had many exotic animals including monkeys and giraffes. My family made a beeline for the two-toed sloth, while I headed to the bathroom. The bathroom was in a nearby barn.

Okay, in all fairness, maybe "barn" was the wrong word as it vaguely reminded me of a camp mess hall from my youth and it had proper plumbing. The camp mess hall was used for all meals, movie nights, and our camp dance that a couple hundred kids attended, so not a small room. I can still picture my camp beau, Johnnie, throwing down his ambitious break-dancing moves to "Smooth Criminal." His Michael Jackson impersonation was complete with a white leather jacket and black loafers that squeaked when he attempted the Moon Walk, sadly he had left his single white glove at home. I watched nearby in my neon skirt, crop top and oversized head scarf that accented my crimped bangs. Wow, those were the days of epic fashion trends! Anyway, I digress back to the barn.

Hidden in the far west corner of the large room was a striking black and white striped 3-month-old baby tiger in a makeshift metal enclosure resembling the one I recently purchased for our new puppy. This "baby" was three times the size of my puppy and I was puzzled by his pen as it would not take much effort for the little guy to escape. I watched the impressive cat for a few minutes before he became aware that I was in the room. The instant magnetism between us felt inherited yet impossible. My sluggish imagination stirred in reaction to his gorgeous cerulean eyes, the rendezvous was nothing short of metamorphosis. I felt as though I was looking at a unicorn, overcome by the sheer magic of the moment. I took one last look at the entrance, walked over, and squatted down beside him without another thought. To say they were understaffed was putting it lightly as in what universe would a regular person be able to get that close to a baby tiger?

I am typically a rule follower, so my next move was very uncharacteristic of me. I climbed over the waist high metal play pen, sat down beside the stunning "kitten" and without warning the little guy climbed into my lap. He sat with me for what felt like an hour and we played and snuggled. He even teethed at my hand which was utterly adorable. I sat there wondering, where is his Mama and why is he in this barn all alone? Tigers (especially those in captivity) are very solitary creatures and perhaps that is what brought us together that day. We both deeply related to the feeling of being alone.

I was twenty-nine years old when I met my tiger friend at the ranch. The visionary tryst stirred something in my soul. I became pensive for several days, considering the potential deeper meaning behind the introspective experience. Holding that baby tiger, sharing an intimate moment as we searched each other's eyes for commonalities was life changing. The whole world was quiet. It was as if some divine entity was throwing me a gift, a lifeline to hold on to with a promise that happier days were ahead. I finally felt as though I had possibilities again. I had not opened my heart up to possibilities for ten years. I was resigned to live the settlement that was my life until that day when I was sparked to contemplate the prospect and possibility of change. Have you ever had an experience that left permanent footprints on your mind, heart, and soul? Footprints that guided you to a new journey ahead and reminded you of the hope discovered in the transformative occasion that is long past? What did the afterglow feel like to you physically? Did you feel tingly all over, did your heart skip a beat, did you have a sudden surge of energy? My exhilarating afterglow and newly discovered awareness of miracles found me beaming like a pageant contestant with her perfect industrial smile. My new shine, after what seemed like an eternity of winters, lit me up with the warm radiance of opportunity, and that kept me faithful. Faithful in this scenario meant that God had a better plan for my life, and it would take time, but soon enough his message would be revealed.

Almost fifteen years have passed since my visit to the ranch, and I still actively search for opportunities to be with tigers and often find profound inspiration in my connection with these fantastic creatures. I attend a conference for our business every other year in Las Vegas and a stop at the Tiger Habitat at the Mirage Resort is always on the agenda. The Tiger Habitat is affiliated with the German American entertainer duo Siegfried & Roy who were known for their magic shows that included lions and tigers back in the 90s. A couple years ago I was able to meet Siegfried who I am told visits his animals every single day. I thanked him for caring for the magnificent tigers and for creating a sacred place to visit with them amongst the bustling party scene of Vegas. Siegfried replied, "We do it together." The genuine kindness in his words and compassion in his eyes dispelled my previous generalized opinion that all keepers of tigers in captivity are doing it for the wrong reasons. He loved those big cats; they were his family.

Siegfried's best friend Roy had been brutally mauled by one of their tigers in a miscommunication during a show in October 2003. Roy barely survived the incident, enduring a severe loss of blood at his neck followed by a stroke. I am astounded that this heroic pair continued to actively love and care for these dangerous animals; it spoke to their selfless character and ability to view life's greater plan. It was an undeniable comparison to my own life-threatening traumas and an ethereal directive to use that wisdom to help others. That realization of opportunity to do something profound with my hardship, serving what I believe to be my life's purpose, made me feel more alive than ever. Like waking up from the best night of sleep of your life, ready to tackle your day with the energy of Captain America. Or hopping off the stool after an invigorating respiratory treatment, Vegas is famous for these, where you feel like you are breathing like Michael Phelps, pumped to swim for the Gold. Energy, clarity, and passion filling up your lungs, oscillating your heart and fueling your brain with new purpose. Roy survived his trauma and lived on for seventeen more years, only passing a couple months ago from complications of the COVID-19 Virus. Our passions and purpose are what keep us alive, against all odds. I believe Roy fought to stay alive because he had a greater purpose and was determined to see it through. I am sure there were many days he just wanted to lay in bed, just as I have, and give up. His story inspires me just as I hope mine will inspire you. You see, my friend, for ten years, I made the choice to live in a deeply pessimistic environment which began to threaten my own persistent positivity. The visit with the baby tiger at the ranch was my first signal that I was living the wrong life.

I am a big believer in signs and symbols, a wake-up call from God or the universe, providing important direction for our lives, especially after life-threatening trauma. I view the tiger as my dominant symbol as I strive to live without fear, overcome obstacles, and lead with courage. I would certainly be remiss if I did not share that part of the relation originates from the red headed Scorpio in me who occasionally must tame strong emotions within myself. The tiger is my tangible symbol of starting each day with a grateful heart and encouraging me to live up to my greatest potential in good times and bad. The tiger represents boundaries, allowing others to be a part of my life with permission and respect. The tiger reminds me when I am feeling small to stand tall and exude confidence. The tiger is resilient, the set back of an illness or personal trauma is short lived and is often followed by a swell of exuberance. The tiger reminds me to be focused and patient as I work toward my goals and achieve my dreams.

Over the last seven years I have interviewed hundreds of management candidates in Virginia and West Virginia for our pizza business. The script of unique questions allows me to evaluate operational experience, core values and leadership aptitude. My favorite question on the list, "If you were an animal, what animal would you be and why?" Recently I asked that question to a seasoned leader with a long military history and his answer struck a chord it me. He paused and his eyes lit up with intense passion as he said, "I would be a tiger as it is always underestimated because the lion is the King of the Jungle." His answer got me thinking about titles. If you google who is stronger, the tiger wins on multiple sites so why does the lion hold the prestigious title? Perhaps it is because the lion fears no other animal? Can you imagine living a life with no fear? Would that be a gift or is a small amount of fear what keeps us grounded and humble? There have been many titles that have landed fear in my heart and soul for my future. The three I would like to share with you today are as follows and are in no particular order.

1. "Unemployed, Divorced, Single Mom."
2. "Rape & Incest Victim."
3. "Cancer Patient."

Living with those titles at the time they were contrived was miserable, but you know what? The traumatic aforementioned titles fueled my fire to fight for the ones I desired, because I had already seen my worst nightmare in every trauma I faced. Looking past trauma, we also must consider the titles we choose to wear that do not reveal our most authentic self. How many times have you made a decision to do something that was all about someone else's goals and then suddenly you are stuck doing something you hate, something that makes you feel like a phony? As a recovering people pleaser, I can tell you it is easy to fall into this web. I am also a proud southerner and the quiet underlying message from adolescence was to always be a polite lady. This does not mean, however, that you have to be a doormat.

I am a big fan of Brené Brown, her books, her TED talks, her humor, her approach to parenting. I love it all. She tells us that, "Authenticity is the daily practice of letting go of who we think we are supposed to be and embracing who we are." How many times in life have you muted who you really are to make someone else more comfortable? I cannot begin to count how many times I have done this but that ends now. I am so excited to share with you how I took my power back by becoming authentic and brave! Committing to authenticity means you have resurfaced at General rank and are no longer afraid of what you have attempted to keep secret for decades. Brave is not even the right adjective for the action of taking your power back after trauma. The only term that comes close, in my humble opinion, is **fierce**. What do you say, are you ready to make a change? Are you ready to see yourself as a fierce survivor instead of a passive victim? We are all victims the moment trauma infiltrates our hearts, minds, and bodies but we ultimately decide how long we allow ourselves to live with that label. I am hopeful that my story will give you the courage and tools to assign yourself the powerful label you deserve after healing from your trauma. For now, try this new mantra on and see how it fits, "I am a fierce survivor and today I am taking my power back. I am no longer a victim!"

My first career after graduate school was working as an opera singer. In my humble opinion, opera is just as much about the costume as it is about the music. The time it takes to be painted, wigged, rigged (corset and all) and tied into your costume, takes about as long as the entire production. When I played Donna Elvira in Mozart's "Don Giovanni" my hair and make-up calls were hours before the first note in the Overture was played. I can still recall the weight of the costume and the pressure to be this character I did not identify with; both were important metaphors for me. It took me several decades to realize that even years past my professional singing career, I was still wearing costumes and playing fictional characters. Donna Elvira screams out at Don Giovanni, "Stay then, barbarian, in your stinking filth, a horrendous example of iniquity," responding to his relentless sarcasm and unfaithfulness. She was not afraid to be authentic and passionate, to say how she really felt no matter how ugly and rejected her display. Drama in an opera is what sells the tickets, and the high notes that break chandeliers! Sadly, when we communicate our truth in dramatic fashion, a product of our passion or our honest-to-goodness selves in real life, it comes across as tragedy and the reviews are devastating. So how do we do it? How do we live faithful truth, face our fears and traumas, and conquer anxiety in our daily lives when all things seem lost or broken? We get out of bed and show up!

My favorite word is serendipity and I have been blessed many times by the occurrence of happy accidents. The serendipitous event of going to that ranch and connecting with a baby tiger ejected me from the submissive ethos of being a victim. That spark landed me back in the driver's seat of my life and my victim mindset slowly became reprogrammed. My once fragile psyche had been reborn in a moment. I would now only view myself as a fierce survivor capable of anything I set my mind to do. I cannot begin to explain how or why God appeared to me through the eyes of a baby tiger that day, but he did. The mandate seemed outrageous, and it took me years to comply, but I did eventually leave my husband. I think many of us make choices that we deem as "forever" situations that we cannot change no matter what the scenario. I would be willing to bet there are countless married people out there who remain in an unhealthy union because they feel they will be punished by a higher power for getting divorced. I was one of those people and I was judged by people I trusted. Being vulnerable to other people's opinions of your impossible decisions is rough but living a lie is so much worse. For years I was going through the motions of my life and providing a very sad example for my children.

Living as a casualty of your life, treading water deep below the surface, instead of the eager dynamo you are capable of becoming is a painful and frustrating experience. Treading water means you stay in the same spot and existing at status quo means you are not growing. When we are not allowing ourselves to thrive in this gift called life, depression sneaks in almost unnoticed. Most of us will be marked by trauma in our lifetime but we have a choice about how we respond to it and how long we live in that depressed state. I lost sight of how to use my voice after the crushing traumas I endured, and depression was easy and constant. God waited for the quiet moment with the tiger to remind me of how to use it again. This book began as a therapeutic exercise to heal from the chronic trauma that tainted two decades of my life; however, during the process I was awakened to my greater purpose, to help others. This book is a gift to you, my friend, as you search for authenticity in your own beautiful voice while healing from the adversity that attempted to define or destroy you. I hope this helps you to be fearless and driven as you live your fiercest, happiest, and very best life today, tomorrow, and always.

Love, Ally

Ally, T.I.G.E.R.S. Preservation Station, 2018

CHAPTER 1
BULLSEYE

The sky revealed a tapestry of white feathers and between the tertiary wings, the sun lit the damp leaf covered pavement in front of me. The rearview mirror featured a fantastic display of fall's offering dancing and spinning in my wake. I was raised in Ellett Valley, a short ten-minute drive from the ambitious tech centered collegiate community of Blacksburg, Virginia, and Virginia Tech University. The scenic drive from town is one that I took for granted for years. I have driven it thousands of times but that day every colorful detail was amplified as my childhood seemed like one, I did not live myself. In a moment my life shifted to reveal two antagonistic dreams. The first dream was my childhood, and the fantastic imagery was intoxicating with no sign of a hangover. The second dream explored the new territory of adversity, which torched my brain with a soul crushing nightmare that poked at me like persistent alcoholism. There was no twelve-step program to heal from the absence of transition or lack of understanding of my new normal.

I had not visited home in a long time but had awoken as an adult overnight. Driving gave me time to think but no quantity of miles would make the pain of loss subside. One day I was a carefree teenager, enjoying a traditional college experience and the next day I was a changed woman with a devastating scar on her unsuspecting heart. As I descended the first country road a corkscrew bend announced a small goat farm, newborn kids trailing adult goats at mealtime. The road leveled out to reveal a hodgepodge of residences, dilapidated single wide trailers, modest red brick ranches and newly erected craftsman homes. In the distance the Allegany Mountains glistened with the first snow of the season, kissing the horizon on a peaceful October morning. Small family farms gave way to expansive dairy farms and as I prepared to make the right turn onto the second country road, the Old Cheese Factory greeted me like an old friend. The label "factory" seemed ironic as the only creature intimidated by the size of the historic building would be a mouse.

As I prepared to make the turn from Harding Avenue to Lusters Gate Road, I thought back to participating in the Virginia Tech "Dairy Show." I was eleven years old and the only responsibility I had in the world was helping to care for a wide eyed, innocent calf named "Babe." An invitation to "intern" with the Virginia Tech dairy department was highly coveted, mainly because the calves were so stinkin' cute! I adored "Babe" and looked forward to our time together but in addition to washing, brushing, and feeding her, I enjoyed the solitude. Even to this day I crave peace and quiet and the simpler days of my pre-teen years where there was nothing to worry about. That Friday I was transformed and hoisted, the weight of the world on my shoulders while I navigated insomnia on a three-hour drive that began before dawn. I paused before making the final turn, realizing in two short minutes I would be home again feeling like a stranger in my life. Trauma had slapped me hard in the face, and I was permanently marked by the news that came from a phone call the night before.

My sister Kiki is a sparkplug, in the best possible way. Seriously y'all, imagine a gorgeous, athletic, petite, blonde-haired, blue-eyed stunner who is great at everything, and I am lucky enough to call her my sister. More important than that, she is also my best friend. I can call her and talk about anything and know that I will leave the call better than when I picked up the phone—that is a gift and one I treasure immensely. Kiki is sincere, trustworthy, unprejudiced, and we always pick up where we left off as though not a day has gone by.

Kiki and I are Irish twins as we were born eleven months apart. We share similar facial features and until our teen years we both suffered through the same bowl cut hair style. I was born with strawberry blonde hair and Kiki, traditional blonde hair. We both had freckles from an early age; although, I had twice as many as Kiki. Some of my favorite memories of the two of us growing up include playing in the creek that separated our neighborhood from a dairy farm, climbing trees near our house, and dancing on the back patio to "Hurt So Good" by John Cougar Mellencamp. We thought we were hot stuff at age five and six pulling up our proper shorts into a "Daisy Duke" look and prancing around while singing at the top of our lungs. My poor parents, I am sure they were mortified. They did manage to capture that "show" on the camcorder, and it later became leverage as we became teenagers and adults with boyfriends, and later our fiancés.

My childhood was a fairytale. Right hand to God, like waking up at Disney but without the lines! My Dad was a physician and surgeon (obstetrician/gynecologist) and my Mom an elementary school teacher who eventually stayed at home with us. Mom and Dad just celebrated their 50th Anniversary last summer and growing up their relationship was my compass for what a happy marriage looked like. They always put each other first, still go on weekly dates, and are instinctively yet organically sweet, like local honey, in their affection for one another. It was obvious to me that God had hand-picked them for one another on one fateful summer day at band camp. Dad was the drum major and Mom, the majorette. I am still convinced she caught his eye with her trendy go-go style marching band boots and the playful tassels that would bounce around when she twirled her baton. I have so many memories from their shared passions when we were kids; morning crossword puzzles over coffee, singing along to Jimmy Buffet songs in the car, sailing on Smith Mountain Lake, searching for seashells on Sunset Beach, reading Stephen King novels the moment they were released, and dancing the night away every chance they got.

Mom & Dad,
early 1960s

The first eighteen years of my life were as happy as I could ever hope them to be. Kiki and I enjoyed swimming and tennis at Blacksburg Country Club. However, our favorite activity in the pool was playing "Sharks & Minnows" in the deep end. We took ballet and jazz dance classes together several times a week, savoring every opportunity to wear too-toos, sequins and glitter. In later years we also took ballroom dancing classes at the University Club at Virginia Tech and sparred over being paired up with one of the few boys with notoriously bad breath. We went to church every Sunday at Northside Presbyterian Church and played hide and seek in the musty basement during youth lock-ins. We traveled to Camp Staunton Meadows in South Boston, VA for two weeks each summer where we learned to boat, ride horses, zip line, and flirt with boys. Halloween was always an event! Mom would help us put together creative costumes that always had an artistic flair thanks to her impressive prowess behind a sewing machine. We attended public schools, made good grades, and had close friends. As high school approached Kiki and I began pursuing individual interests and did not have as much in common. Kiki was a cheerleader and skilled runner; her track event was hurtling. She was also a natural equestrian and competed in jumping events all over Virginia.

Kiki & Ally:
Halloween 1989

I was not much of an athlete and decided to pursue music, learning to play piano from a woman in our neighborhood who was infamous for smacking your knuckles if you did not practice. When I turned thirteen, I began playing flute and took voice lessons, along with piano. In high school I was a member of the Symphonic Band and the Madrigal Singers, a Renaissance acapella singing group. One of my favorite parts about being a madrigal singer was, the dress! Mom and I made the thirty-minute drive to Schoolhouse Fabrics in Floyd, VA. We enthusiastically climbed the three stories of the historic schoolhouse and perused room after room of every texture and pattern of fabric you can imagine. It was like a treasure hunt, except the gold we found was soft to the touch and flattering to the figure! After several hours we chose teal velvet, ivory silk, and maroon, gold, and teal trim to construct a gorgeous period gown with a matching flat top veiled Medieval head dress. Our group was invited to sing all over the community, and I loved every opportunity to wear that costume no matter what the season or weather.

I also performed in the flag corps with our award-winning Blacksburg High School Marching Band. Picture red headed, flute toting Michelle from *American Pie* without the weird sexual innuendos. I did actually march with my flute the first year before committing the final three years to the flag corps. Now imagine marching band was cool because in my day and age, it was! I loved every minute of the marching band culture; Friday night football games, half-time routines, wearing culottes and beret hats, and Saturday competitions in Chilhowie, VA. Those were my people and laughter was always close by when we were all together. No one ever says this, but high school was a dream as I had friends in all cliques, went to dances with nice boys and avoided what little drama there was. As a senior I won singing competitions, was crowned Spring Festival Queen, and was accepted early decision for my first-choice college. Life was good! I also met my first love in high school, and it was as if I was following Mom and Dad's playbook page by page and line by line.

I had a few dates in middle and high school before meeting the man I refer to as "my first love." I was definitely not everyone's type as a "Carrot Top" redheaded, freckle faced late bloomer. I had my share of rejections before and after the man I am about to tell you about. The experience of loving that man did not abolish the possibility of rejection, it just showed me what kismet looked like. I understood the fundamental existence of a kindred spirit, a match so perfect that it had to be created by God. The experience of being loved for everything you are, including your flaws, gives us hope and I believe God gives us the good fortune to meet more than one kindred spirit over a lifetime.

Do you recall your first passion, the first activity or interest that set your soul on fire? Music was my first passion, however; my second passion could have been its twin as my zeal for it was just as rich. I was already hinting at it when I told you about my teal velvet Renaissance gown. My second passion took up residence in my heart on a rainy day in September my sophomore year of high school. I had enrolled in a fashion merchandising class on a whim and that first day of class it was as though a flame was ignited in me. I was ecstatic and could not wait to learn more about fashion marketing and trends. I had already dived deep into current trends without a paddle, embracing short plaid skirts, baby tees, chokers, and platform boots. I was completely submerged, and the newly discovered passion changed the way I looked at the world. I had acquired a new accessory, and it was better than the most stylish Kate Spade specks. I now viewed the world through an intuitive lens, attentive to every subtle nuance of fashion. I had a new filter for which I observed movies, magazines, and department store displays and it was fantastically fun! I was always working part time jobs from the time I was fifteen and that limited disposable income was always—and I mean always—devoted to fashion.

Week two of fashion merchandising class I received the gift of my life—well, at least up until that point. Ms. Agee walked to the front of our classroom, confidently clicking her two-inch Calvin Klein red pumps. She turned and revealed matching red lips positioned in a telling smile, holding a secret that was sure to create a frenzy. Ms. Agee was beautiful but also so humble and impressively authentic. I remember thinking I hope I can be as sophisticated as she is when I become an adult. Ms. Agee's gorgeous auburn locks were pulled halfway back, revealing her striking blue eyes, that were fixed on a single piece of paper she held in her right hand. She asked us to quiet down, quickly reviewed the memorandum once more, and then invited the entire class to visit the Merchandise Mart in Atlanta. The Merchandise Mart was comprised of five floors, one hundred thirty showrooms, and eight thousand brands and was not open to the public. It was the chance of a lifetime! I was so excited that I scurried out of the classroom to tell my friends and ran headfirst into him. I could not be sure if the intense flutter in my chest was the afterglow from the thrilling invitation or God's alarm clock that I had met my "first love."

I still remember our first date like it was yesterday. Eric arrived at my house in his 'suped up' Toyota truck that required a foot stool to get into. Yes, it was a little country, but that sweet boy could have arrived on a dirt bike, and I would have gladly hopped on. When you grow up in Southwestern Virginia you roll the dice when it comes to introducing your date to your family. I have heard stories of mud-covered cowboy boots ruining the entry rug or a casual drop of a lesser-known slang phrase like "buffalo scared" and suddenly no one is good enough for their little girl. Or an ill-timed chuckle about a *back country* private joke that leaves both you and your beau flushed. By the way, I am not clear on what "buffalo scared" even means but believe it relates to buffalos genetic memory and general fear of lions and tigers. I secretly loved bold fashion moves like cowboy boots and flannel shirts, it was honest and represented the home I loved. When Eric opened the truck door for me that night there was a single red rose waiting for me on my seat. The gift of the partially opened, delightfully fragrant red rose is probably the most romantic gesture I have ever received on a first date...well, except for a surprise pizza party in 2011 but more on that later.

This was my very first date with a boy picking me up; all previous dates involved a ride from my Dad to the mall. I remember "Water Runs Dry" by Boyz II Men was on the radio as we pulled out of the driveway. Eric was without a doubt showing me "the water" as the vast desert of bad dates that awaited me in the future would leave me thirsty and disappointed. I was so thankful for his genuine kindness, innate respect, and unmatched chivalry. I wish I could transport that level of honor and reverence to the current dating model in high school where 50% of the guys require "nudes" before they will ask a girl on a date. Forget about meeting the parents at the door—all you hear is a distant honk of the horn. I have six daughters and some of their stories and their friends' stories bring on panic attacks as it feels so transactional.

Eric stood 5'10" with blonde hair and green eyes. He was an only child, but you would never know it, there was no evidence that he had been spoiled. He was selfless, and I admired the way he took care of his parents, our friends, and me. The sensual attraction between us was exhilarating yet I always felt completely respected. Eric's lips were deliciously full and enraptured mine sending an electric tinge through my entire body. Falling in love was easy and uncomplicated with Eric. Our hearts were pure, unjaded by love's heart break that leaves their casualties wounded. Being able to love freely without replaying the film from your past mistakes was a gift although I never realized it was such until I had been bruised and battered by love several years later. Eric and I were writing the script of our love story with fresh, impartial eyes, and it was wonderful.

Eric enjoyed working on cars and was a very talented artist. I loved to watch him create art, his muscular hands carefully sketching, his brow slightly furrowed with intense concentration as he committed memory to paper. One sunny afternoon my visit interrupted his meticulous creation of a rattle snake, coiled up, ready to strike. The life like image made my skin crawl as poisonous snakes were a regular part of our reality in Southwest Virginia. His mother opened the door and invited me into their home that day and as I slipped down the basement steps unnoticed, I admired his focus and how his eyes spoke with passion and intensity before his lips parted. Our mediums of artistic expression were different, but our passion for the gift to create, the same.

Eric worked at a local grocery store, and I would drive over and visit with him on his breaks. We would sit, hand in hand, on the hood of his car, listening to music while looking at the stars. Silently I thanked God for this man and the many ways he showed his love for me, as I gazed at the night sky of distant lights above me. My first experience with love was a dream and I made a lot of naïve assumptions about the typical dating experience that were soon chased away. Eric would surprise me with love notes written on actual paper, that came from a living tree. Now a days you are lucky to get a heart emoji as a tribute of your man's affection. Eric would create playlists of our favorite songs on cassette tapes and pass them to me between a crowd of classmates before the bell rang. Eric would meet me before and after school ensuring that whatever happened in between was tolerable because I always had the shelter of his love to brighten my bad days. I was convinced that God had given me the gift he had given my parents, a promising future with my first love. My most treasured memory with him was the night he took me to my junior prom.

Eric & Ally, Junior Prom 1993

My sweet Mama let me splurge on a gorgeous white dress with emerald satin on the underside of the train and a bodice accented with pearls and green crystal beading. I wore my long red hair down and curled, it cascaded over the spaghetti straps like a cape. Eric wore a black tuxedo with an emerald bow tie and cummerbund woven with gold paisleys that matched my dress. I felt like a princess and remember hoping the night would never end. Eric took me to a fancy French dinner before the dance at La Maison. This was the nicest restaurant within a 100-mile radius of my home, and I ordered a roasted chicken entrée with a decadent raspberry sauce and haricots vert. Every aspect of the night was so perfectly planned and orchestrated, and I remember feeling so grateful for a perfect prom as I danced the night away to all of our favorite songs.

We attended the after-prom party at the local recreation center, where we played basketball, ate pizza, and chatted with friends. As the perfect evening crept toward dawn, it was time to go home. The song "Come Undone" by Duran Duran was popular at that time and as Eric drove me home that night it was playing. It is a somber tune as it very clearly talks about loss or trauma and who you depend on when that experience occurs. It was almost as if the lyrics were foreshadowing events that would occur in the coming year. It is interesting how a song can transport you back to an earlier time and suddenly you feel every emotion and physical sensation from that time as if it were yesterday. I cannot help but think about Eric each time I hear a Boyz II Men or Duran Duran song. That season of my life was more than twenty years ago, but my heart still beats a little faster and my breath is slightly arduous whenever those songs play. It is all so fresh again for a fleeting moment, and the pain and joy of those memories is both a blessing and a curse.

My parents moved to Ocean Isle Beach last year. When they were packing, they discovered my junior prom dress in the back of a closet, just as beautiful as the day we bought it. The dress almost felt bridal with the elegant train and regal adornments. They say your wedding day is supposed to be the happiest day of your life, the dress, the venue, the food and of course, the groom. As a Christian, I believed you only got the one day as I did not believe in divorce. For years I romanticized what that kind of happy would look and feel like on my perfect wedding day. As I think back on my wedding day, it was not the happiest. Far from the happiest in fact. After the marriage ended, I remember thinking about that prom dress, the prom, and my prince. I remember feeling so beholden to God to be given the gift of that perfect day, and a perfect milestone event (the prom) with Eric, and now the memories to look back upon. It was the memory of my fairytale prom night with Eric that helped me survive the fact that my wedding and honeymoon experiences started with a panic attack before walking down the aisle and ended in tears returning from our honeymoon. I had built my perfect wedding experience happiness up so much in my mind that it almost felt like a death and the morning after our honeymoon ended, I was grieving. I would bet that many women have felt this way. It is so easy to get caught up in romanticizing the engagement and wedding event that sometimes we do not take a good hard look at whether or not we chose the right groom. In my case, I jumped into a fresh relationship in utter denial, hiding from the sexual trauma of the one before it. My failed marriage was just as much my fault as I was in no position to pick a life partner but more on that later.

Eric and I made the decision to take a break before starting college as he was a year older, and I was planning to go to college in North Carolina. I always believed in my heart that we would get back together when we could be in the same place again. God always gave me subtle cues when I was invited to a party at his college or when I saw him in traffic when I was home at Christmas my freshman year. I kept thinking; you have time and there is no rush. I did not realize that God was potentially giving me an opportunity to change the future. I was not listening; I did not believe anything bad could happen because nothing bad had ever happened before. I was blissfully unaware of tragedy, living my very protected happy existence in a world where everything seemed to go as planned.

One year later my Dad called me out of the blue. He had called me multiple times, but I was away from my apartment. I had gone to the North Carolina Fall Festival in Raleigh with some of the girls from my music sorority. When I finally got home after too much popcorn and cotton candy, the phone was ringing again. I stumbled over my bed and snatched the phone receiver on the last ring. I remember thinking that the ring sounded haunting, and I found myself startled by the bright blinking off the retro spotlight phone in an otherwise dark room. My knee was throbbing, having grazed the bed's footboard, and after a moment of silence, I heard my dad's voice. "Ally? Is that you?" Dad's strong baritone voice was broken, and I had never heard him so vulnerable. "I have some very hard news," he finally clamored, his voice quivering. "Eric was driving back to school late last night," he paused, his breath clumsy. "He was hit head on by a drunk driver," he gasped. "He was killed instantly." The impossible news discharged a wrecking ball and the cold forged steel flattened me with all its fury. I was not equipped to withstand it and just like that, my life was forever changed.

So, when I said my sister is good at everything, she is! Kiki is an impressive athlete, respected female leader who has climbed the corporate ladder in a male dominated industry, trusted friend, and follower of Jesus. In her spare time, she loves to travel, surf, hike, and she hunts large bears with a cross bow. Kiki is listed on the National Hunting Register for her record-breaking conquest of a 444 lb. black bear, taken in Saskatchewan, Canada. She named the bear "Bruiser." Bruiser's impressive stature is memorialized in her basement in Kansas. I have tried to imagine her exhilarating yet terrifying experience many times. The day of the hunt, my brave 5'2" sister climbed a tree dressed head to toe in camo, she waited patiently for the precise shot for hours and had to remain perfectly still. I could not comprehend the fact that a missed attempt would certainly risk her life as bears are fully adept to climb trees. Her story is the definition of courage, and one of the reasons I love and respect her so much.

Now imagine being "Bruiser," innocently walking through the forest, ignorant to what is happening above him in the trees. Suddenly he feels a sharp pain and feverishly thrashes between anger, fear, confusion, and uncertainty. Little did he know he had become a bullseye and his life, although short, was never going to be the same. I felt like the bear, hit without warning, except I felt as if hundreds of razor-sharp arrows had entered my flesh. My heart no longer felt like a muscle, capable of operating the machine that was my body. It felt like a decaying organ, one that would need a transplant. I could not imagine loving anything or anyone with my ruined heart. Part of me died that day not only because I lost my first love but also my perception of the world had changed in a moment. I had endured my first trauma at the age of nineteen, and sadly it was only the first of many to come. I dropped the phone, grabbed my keys, and ran out to my car. I drove, without a destination, in the pouring rain listening to our playlist on a sad, barely functional cassette tape. Fleeing in my car would soon become a pattern, attempting to outrun the impossible news that had quickly become my reality.

As I think back on that time today, I feel incredibly thankful for my family who carried me through that devastating time. My sister drove me to the funeral and held my shaking body as I cried for my love and mourned my broken dreams of a future with him. I was able to say goodbye, placing my hand delicately on his hand and gazing upon his handsome face in the open casket. Eric's face was bruised and swollen from the car accident, the deathly sight of him was inconceivable to process. His skin was so cold, his body hard, he looked like an elegant statue preserved on perfect white satin. He was gone and it was so final. My window to be with him was closed, boarded, and abandoned. The last time I spoke to him was in the band hallway at our high school less than a year before. A mutual friend invited him to one of my performances as a surprise. There was still something between us, even then, recalling the warmth of his touch and the surrender of my body into his strong arms when he hugged me hello. I still had a chance to be his, and him mine. I believed I would one day marry this man and the loss made me feel as though I was dying, and I no longer understood the feeling or action of hope. I could not imagine conjuring up the energy to continue the path toward my dreams, as a big part of my future was now just a series of memories.

I had grown up protected from adversity and seeing how cruel the world could be was a tough pill to swallow. The sobering reality is that life will always include periods of crisis and loss. I read a powerful quote by football coach Lou Holtz, "Life is 10% what happens to me and 90% how I react to it." I do not have absolute power to eliminate pain and heartbreak; however, I do have a deeply supportive foundation of a loving, nurturing family. The point is I could choose to be all consumed by my hardship and succumb to a deep depression or I could allow myself to grieve and be grateful for the time I had with him. I chose the latter and leaned on my family and the Lord. I visited his gravesite many times in the weeks and months that followed, watching butterflies and bees frolic in nearby flowers. I began to feel peace and let go of the resentment that his life had been cut tragically short by a horrible decision another person chose to make. I knew in my heart he was with God, living it up in heaven, and no longer in pain. Thankfully when I look at my life today, I realize that God had a reason for those unanswered prayers and the sting of loss has dulled considerably. I still think about the feathery sky that God revealed to me on the drive home to Eric's funeral.

In Isaiah 43:2 the Bible tells us, "He will cover you with his feathers, and under his wings you will find refuge." There are no accidents, God painted that sky and published that scripture before my eyes when he knew I needed it most and the message was very clear: I was not alone. The other message, which was not translated until many years later, there is more than one kindred spirit. You may end up with the first one or the first one may just show you what pure love looks like and how to identify it. Eric showed me exactly what I needed to be looking for and although it took me fifteen more years to find him, I did find him and have never been happier.

Dad, Ally, Kiki, and Mom, 2019

LIFE LESSON #1
Begin each day with a grateful heart, a
morning routine, go outside and get
centered!

My first life lesson I share with you, my friend, is to develop a gratitude practice along with a meaningful morning routine, go outside and get centered. Wow, life lesson #1 makes me sound like a bossy smarty-pants but I promise, it is not as daunting as it seems. During some of the darkest days of my life I was still able to find at least a handful of things to be grateful for. Each morning I wake up and begin my quiet time with gratitude for the many blessings in my life. The focus on the positive gives me strength and courage to move forward and realize that the crisis at hand is only temporary and better days are ahead.

My morning routine was conceived from two influences, "War Room" by Chris Fabry and "The Miracle Morning" by Hal Elrod. Both books gave me great ideas of how to set up each day for success. The first thing I did was create a prayer retreat (or quiet time retreat) in my home. I have a large walk-in closet that a previous homeowner used as a craft room. I took one corner of the room and devoted it to my daily quiet time. I went to Home Goods and bought a $10 framed cork board and created a goal board and prayer road map if you will. I made the board colorful with sticky notes of my favorite bible verses, positive affirmations, and pictures that represented current goals. I added an ottoman for comfort and several devotional books for daily inspiration and focus. Each morning my day begins with brushing my teeth, washing my face, followed by my quiet time in the prayer retreat. I begin with deep, diaphragmatic breathing to get centered, followed by the long list of blessings I am grateful for. If I need a boost, I recite positive affirmations until I feel more confident. The devotional books are structured to read one per day and are labeled with each day of the year. If you are not into devotionals, there are plenty of positive quote books on Amazon that should help you to create that positive mindset before you begin your work day. I spend a minimum of thirty minutes in the quiet space and miraculously my days are always super productive and satisfying when I devote that time. I have become a more patient and present mom to my kids, a more attentive and affectionate wife, and a better focused leader for my team. My fully focused quiet time has truly changed my life and allows me to make better daily decisions and be more balanced in mind, body, and spirit.

I mentioned before that the cognitive realization of hardship stings almost as much as the loss itself. I often felt like my peers did not understand me and seemed uncomfortable when I became lost in pensive thoughts. It felt hopeless trying to navigate the dark labyrinth that had become my life, and those simple days of playing with calves in a quiet barn seemed like a hundred lifetimes ago. I could not figure out how to reconnect to those simple, happy days of my youth and felt worn-down by the burden of misery. Sitting on the couch, consumed by my depression was not a place I could stay for long—I had to take action. I have always loved being outside and began doing some soul searching on how to connect the fairytale of my childhood with the hard reality of my late-teen years. I thought about activities I used to enjoy doing outside and remembered how therapeutic and restorative the fresh air and sunshine had been at the beach. I live more than five hours from the beach so a trip there would require a plan; however, picking up my tennis racket again was something I could easily do. It is also a great stress reliever, hitting that fuzzy little yellow ball. Now tennis may not be your thing but there are other activities you could choose to do outside like walking, throwing the ball for your dog, playing basketball, or riding a bike. Thirty minutes of vitamin D and fresh air can make a world of difference, trust me. Try it today and watch how your mood is positively affected by this small tweak to your routine. I also do a lot of walking for my mental health, and to stay active. I crave it actually and have gotten to the point where I will make it happen no matter what the weather. It only takes two minutes to buy a full-length poncho from the Dollar Store and removing the excuses really put an extra spring in my step!

These ideas may seem overwhelming, but you can start smaller. Maybe you just commit to five minutes of prayer or positive affirmations after brushing your teeth or a ten-minute walk after dinner. I have learned that when we are grieving after trauma, we must set realistic expectations. When I first began my morning routine, I had a list of very specific requirements, and that list was long. I never allowed enough time to scratch the surface of that list and I always felt disappointed. The feeling of disappointment always overshadowed the connection I was making with what I was reading or praying about. I had to break it down. I also had to mix up my routine at times. For instance, if you wake up feeling down, maybe you had a bad dream or did not get enough sleep, you may need to punt. If I wake up feeling that way, I put on my Nikes and go out for a walk first thing.

While walking I take long, deep breaths and take notice of nature waking up around me. I watch the Robins collecting materials for their nest or the baby bunnies eating the grass nearby. Breathing in the fresh air and getting my body moving provides a great organic reset for me. Once I feel more grounded, I can start talking to God during my morning walk. The feeling of disappointment became an important trigger for me, I had to change up my routine to work through a budding new season of anxiety. There is usually a choice when you are creating a new routine and not everyone prefers the same environment for their quiet time. If you do not have a walk-in closet, go get centered on the porch or in your kitchen before your family gets up. It can feel intimidating to start a new practice but there are no rules. Block that "you" time on your calendar, start designing a routine and brew a pot of coffee while you are at it. God wants to hear from you and more than that, he wants to help you!

I told you that I typically spend a minimum of thirty minutes in quiet time, but it did not start that way. When I kicked off my morning routine, I was still in the practice of cluttering up my calendar with too many commitments. The morning routine did not begin as priority number one. It was usually the calendar appointment that got bumped to the next day, and the next day, and the day after that. I had to start smaller. I wanted my morning routine to work but putting a thirty-minute commitment on it initially was an unrealistic expectation. I decided to start with five minutes. In those five minutes I read one scripture and prayed for everyone on my prayer list. Once I had the five minutes set in stone, I added five more minutes and was able to include a gratitude practice for all the many ways God has blessed my life. I continued to add five minutes at a time until I got up to my goal of thirty minutes. I was listening to self-help guru, Tony Robbins recently. He shared, "When you are grateful, fear disappears and abundance appears." As a person who has struggled with anxiety and fear for two decades, this was a powerful reminder.

I also set my day up for success with resources. Inevitably we all oversleep now and then and start the dreaded morning dash the minute our feet hit the floor. This happened to me a lot when I was suffering the new manifestation of sorrow from fresh trauma and sleep was easy. I had to find a solution because not talking to God would make my bad situation worse. I came up with an idea while walking around an airport during a layover. The airport gift shops have a variety of reading materials no matter what your interest might be. I also discovered that they have a great selection of devotionals and positivity books. I have found devotionals that are geared for moms, wives, young women, college students, couples, men, and individuals who are over stressed or charged with anxiety. There are also devotionals that can be done in three minutes, five minutes, or longer. Many of us fall into multiple categories. I decided to remove my excuses and purchased two devotional books, one for my prayer retreat and one for my car. By eliminating your excuses and structuring a plan that allows you to achieve that first morning goal no matter how the day starts means that disappointment begins to dissipate. It really does not matter where or how much time you spend with God, centering yourself for the day, just as long as you have a couple of minutes. When I am short on time and rushing to my first commitment of the day, I can still take a couple of minutes to read the scripture for the day in the car devotional book. Once I have read my daily devotion, I start up the car and talk to God while driving to my first meeting. Granted, I get some weird looks here and there but over the years I realized that I really do not care what strangers in traffic think of me. I just smile and wave.

Do you worry about what others are thinking about you? Not just in the car while talking to God, but in other areas of your life as well? Does it affect your inner dialogue and how you feel about yourself? We must be careful about that inner dialogue that often includes labeling ourselves as a failure. Feeling like a failure is only going to keep you buried in that melancholy frame of mind, trapped under the covers of your comfy bed. Change your language to one of self-love. Instead of saying, "Darn it, I did not do my five minutes of quiet time this morning...I am a failure," you enthusiastically proclaim, "I did two minutes of quiet time while making my coffee and I feel great!" Remember what I said in the Intro about changing your mindset from victim to survivor. Going through the motions of life is living as a victim but it only takes one moment to put your foot down and boldly proclaim, "Today, I am turning over a new leaf as a survivor." Starting a new journey as a survivor means you are in charge of how you show up in mind, body, and spirit each day. Yesterday your trauma attempted to take you down but today, you are in control of your time and thoughts! I hope the gift of time and personal growth reinvigorate your soul, my friend. You deserve a daily prelude that reignites your energy and passion for life! You have got this!

CHAPTER 2
THE "C" WORD

I died in the Spring of 1997. I became lost in a vivid nightmare, a hideous hallucination, swept away by an aggressive current that was no match for my defeated body. I believed it was the end. The water shattered the hospital bathroom sink with its fury and suddenly it was all around me. I could not breathe, my vision became dark, and then the morphine kicked in and I was a stranger to all who knew me. As my pastor left the hospital room in tears, I prepared for the worst.

Three months earlier…

It was the second Saturday in March, my Mom's 50th Birthday and my Dad was cooking up a seafood feast, sautéed Shrimp Newburg served in puffed pastry, accompanied by roasted asparagus, and whipped potatoes. The main event was followed with a fancy Chateaux Briand cake from our favorite French style local bakery. Kiki and her boyfriend were home, and I was in from college. It had been six months since Eric passed and I was still having hard days, but they were becoming fewer. I was acting as Dad's sous chef but just a standby ready to grab items he needed during his creative culinary process. I found myself daydreaming. Dad was very focused on absolute perfection for my Mom's special day and was not chatty.

Before I returned home, I had just finished staging a new production of Gian Carlo Menotti's Opera, "The Telephone." The two-person cast, comedic opera had been such fun to develop with my friend and opera professor, Joyce. We recruited my church job singing buddy, Tim, to play the male role. As a classically trained singer many of my peers and I took church jobs where we were paid to be soloists and lead our voice part in the chorus at local churches. It was not a lot of money but for the three hours a week required time commitment it was a nice ratio. Tim reminded me of the character David from the show *Schitt's Creek* with his compelling wit, easy humor, and twenty-four-carat heart. I admired how he left judgement at the door and embraced people from all walks of life which was not always the case as we were living in the middle of the Bible Belt. We had a lot of laughs the three of us and I was excited to get back so we could take the production on the Road. Joyce arranged for Tim and me to perform at other North Carolina colleges in addition to Elon, where I attended college.

I had been home for over a week before Mom's Birthday. It was March and a strange golf ball sized mass had taken up residence on my neck a couple of months before. Dad had scheduled a few more doctors' appointments and a biopsy to rule out anything scary earlier in the week. There is a running joke that doctor's daughters are often cursed with numerous health afflictions and I had been included in this ill-fated category but did not see the punchline. I had endured countless ear infections and illnesses which lead to the removal of my tonsils at age five. When I was eight, I broke my ankle while skipping in the hallway at school. At age twelve I was experiencing double vision which led to eye muscle surgery resulting in a two-week diabolical, red-eyed stare that scared my Grandma Josephine. Finally, my gift for starting high school was a twenty-five-degree curvature of my spine and a Boston scoliosis brace that had to be worn twenty-three hours a day. But all those experiences were child's play compared to the news I was about to receive.

I looked over after I finished cutting the asparagus and Dad had left the kitchen. He did not seem like himself, but I wrote it off as intense concentration and nothing more. The kitchen was in the center of the first floor of our home and included a small dining area, French doors led out to a charming screened-in porch accented with a variety of plants and a comfy seating area that invited you out for morning coffee. Surrounding the kitchen was a large family room, dining room, and living room that we used as a music room. The living room was elegant. Ivory valances framed three windows; two teal upholstered love seats faced each other with a perfect view of the baby grand piano. The romantic space allowed me to imagine a scene where Mozart entertained a group of wealthy friends, by candlelight on the forte piano in the 1780s. Mom studied piano and was always agreeable to play accompaniment as I learned a new oratorio or opera role. My sweet Mama has music resounding from her soul. Unknowingly, she expels an enchanting hum that can only be interpreted as wholehearted contentment. I call her "hummingbird" and hope she realizes it is my highest compliment as effortless serenity has always been a dream of mine. I do not remember her being stressed or burdened very often as a child, she was the definition of easygoing and kindhearted. Unless you mention President Trump but that is another story.

In the back of the house, behind the kitchen was a den that comprised an impressive library of Mom and Dad's fiction and horror collections, with a few medical books. We called that room the library, and even now when I walk in there, I get the chills. "Ally, can you help me in here please?" my Dad called out from the library. I walked in and did not see him at first, his back was facing me, the room was completely dark. I asked him what I could do to help him. "You can help me cry," he bellowed, his face soaked with fresh tears. I do not recall ever seeing my Dad cry except at a funeral. He pulled me into a hug and a million things went through my head. Who died? Is he sick, or my Mom? Had he lost his job? What? His explanation was the last thing I thought I would ever hear from his trembling lips. "Ally, you have cancer," he finally blurted out. My body went limp, and he held me as I tried to wrap my mind around the new information. I could not even cry, I was absolutely stunned.

After what seemed like hours, Dad and I emerged from the library. We found Mom and Kiki in the family room sharing a laugh. It felt like two different movies were being played in our home, a comedy in the family room and a horror in the library. None of them had any idea of my diagnosis as Dad was our protector and suffered in solitude over tough news to spare the rest of us. Dad, with his arm around me, shared my medical status and the night was ruined. I remember feeling heartbroken, like I had sabotaged my Mom's milestone birthday. My Granddaddy Frank, Mom's Dad, had just passed a couple months before and now her first born had cancer. Not a great year for my Mom to say the least. Unfortunately, Dad had no choice with the timing as the pathology report had come back that day and on the following day we would leave for the University of Virginia hospital for a week of tests to determine treatment.

Mom, Dad, and I arrived at UVA around eleven on a Monday morning. UVA was only two and a half hours from our home in Blacksburg; it was a beautiful sunny day and I tried to compartmentalize my worries and enjoy the drive. We arrived at the hospital and began the long walk to the UVA oncology department. I was taken to a room, given a hospital gown, and was told my team would soon be in to talk with me. My medical team of four doctors, a mix of attending and resident physicians, joined the three of us in the cold, sterile room. I was warned it would be a long week of tests but that we would have a game plan by the end, and I would be able to go home for treatment. The only question I could muster was, "Will I lose my hair?" Three out of the four doctors looked at the floor; one brave female doctor looked at me and nodded. Her compassion was solid, she had mastered the subtle art of a refined bedside manner.

I searched her kind brown eyes for reassurance and as she returned my glance with slight dismay, I finally unleashed it all. My face looked like a furious tsunami that not even an entire box of Kleenex could remedy, my voice clamoring in all three octaves as I grasped for breath, terrified of the unknown.

Ok Mamas, we all know that childbirth is at the top of the list of most painful experiences ever. One of my tests during this ordeal rivaled childbirth if you can believe it. To get a firm diagnosis of the exact type of cancer I had, the doctors had to perform a bone marrow biopsy and that is not easy to retrieve. The technician took what seemed like the biggest needle I, or anyone, had ever seen and drove it into my tailbone to get the sample, while my Dad held both of my hands for support and so I would not run away. I screamed loud, like opera singer breaks a glass, kind of loud. I envisioned being shot at close range and would choose childbirth without an epidural any day over that. It was soon over, and we returned to my room, me with a very sore backside.

My Mom is an expert shopper and the one bright spot in this whole nightmare was the many ways she and my Dad tried to lift my spirits. She greeted Dad and me after the bone marrow biopsy with an armful of shopping bags. She had bought out the Victoria Secret of their most beautiful, satin pajama sets. They were soft and luxurious and one of them had colorful fish all over it and made me think of being at Sunset Beach again. I guess they thought that being in a hospital would not suck as much if I were wearing something cute. My Mom and Dad have the most beautiful, loving hearts and I am eternally grateful to them for caring for me in every way imaginable as I fought for my life.

During an ordeal like this you also learn who your true friends are. I received boxes and boxes of letters, cute hats, and scarves in a variety of styles. I also received thoughtful care packages from family and friends every week for several months. Our family friend and neighbor, Carol, made a scarf "anchor" that almost looked like a headband with a Velcro strap to keep my fashion forward scarves from sliding off my head. My band director, Dr. Love, visited with an arsenal of homeopathic remedies to battle my spinal headaches. Her last name was truly a testament to her beautiful soul. I also had many visitors at our home and weekly calls from family and friends. Several of my high school friends visited me in the hospital with chocolate treats and warm hugs. Joyce sent me a post card or letter with a funny animal on it every single day from North Carolina to make me laugh. Joyce was like a second mother to me and kept me strong with her unwavering optimism and delightful humor. I also had three other very special friends from Elon that provided miraculous support. Dr. Bragg and Mary Alice were able to arrange for my tuition to be refunded and they treated me like the daughter they never had. With their help and support I was also able to graduate on time and create a top-notch senior recital even though I missed an entire semester (more on this later.) I also discovered I had a brother from another mother in Jimmy during this whole ordeal. He was a guitar major, and we were in side-by-side dorms our freshman year. We had many classes together and I cannot exactly explain it, but he has always felt like family and his compassion for my traumas over the years is unmatched. I had a support army lining up for me, it was time to get my mind strong and ready for battle.

At the end of that first week, we had our final answers and a plan. I was diagnosed with Burkitt's Lymphoma, a form of Non-Hodgkin's Lymphoma, that is associated with impaired immunity and is rapidly catastrophic if not treated quickly. Burkitt's Lymphoma is very rare and was originally discovered in the 50s in Africa. The young African children's cases were related to an Epstein-Barr infection which transformed infected B-cells into cancer cells. It was a mystery how I had developed this specific, and very rare type of Lymphoma but there was no time for further research, it was time to prepare for a big fight. The team determined that my best course of treatment would be intense chemotherapy for five hours a day for three weeks at a time, one week off, for three months. I was also scheduled for monthly spinal taps as Burkitt's Lymphoma tends to travel to the brain after originating in the lymph nodes in the neck. The UVA oncology team ordered the big guns, Adriamycin, and Methotrexate. To administer Methotrexate, the nurse must be covered from head to toe in protective, non-corrosive medical gear. Imagine Renee Russo's character in "Outbreak" and they were going to put that lethal cocktail in my veins?! My veins were impossible, it always took multiple sticks to get any blood, so I was scheduled to have a port-a-cath surgically implanted for my treatments. The port-a-cath is a small metal and rubber circular device that is connected to a vein in the chest. It is placed under but near the surface of the skin and can be accessed with a small needle for chemo. It sounds horrific but it is a much better solution when you have an intense chemo schedule the way I did. I was acquiring a collection of impressive scars in a matter of weeks. The first from the initial neck biopsy and partial removal of the tumor on the left side of my neck and the second two inches below my collar bone on the right side of my chest. Sadly, the partial tumor removal also left me with minor nerve damage. The upside is that the left side of my neck is forever an instrumental participant in foreplay with the pins and needles sensation that has dwindled over time, which is a gift to my husband, ha ha!

Over the course of the week of tests my parents and I were able to come up with a comprehensive list of questions for the UVA oncology team so we would be ready to return home to begin treatment. The two answers I got stuck on…

Chemotherapy would cause me to be very sick (nausea and vomiting were hard to manage during chemo at that time.)

I would likely never be able to have children.

I do not remember saying anything on the almost three-hour drive home. You see, friends, having babies was what I wanted most in the world, even singing took a back seat to that dream and now that dream was dead. All I could think about was in the last six months I had lost Eric, my Granddaddy, and I now had cancer and would never be a Mama. I also remember my Dad saying, "Ally, if you die, I will never believe in God again." Where was God? Why was all of this happening? What had I done to deserve all of this? What was I to learn from all of this? The three of us were beaten down physically, emotionally, and mentally. We got home late and retired early as the next day I would start chemotherapy.

There have been many movies made in the last ten years that have allowed us a peak into what a chemotherapy treatment room looks like. At that time, however, I had no idea what I was about to get into. The UVA team had placed me into the very capable hands of the oncology team at Blue Ridge Cancer Care in Blacksburg. It was there that I met two angels, Dr. McCoy and Nurse Jan who would be attempting to kill my cancer and save my life over the next few months. Jan would always greet us with a reassuring smile and handled the ugliness of my chemo reactions with such heartfelt humanity and professionalism. Neither Dr. McCoy nor Jan ever made me feel like I would not make it through the grueling cancer treatments, they kept me strong and positive. It takes a very special person to commit to a career in cancer care and I knew I had met two of the best.

The first few weeks were awful, beyond my comprehension of the horror that is chemotherapy. The nausea led to extreme, daily vomiting. I was very sensitive to smells which also led to vomiting. The spinal taps led to excruciating spinal headaches. The gruesome effects of the chemo left large sores in my mouth and throat. I was unable to eat real food and was forced to drink Ensure, also known as the nastiest liquid protein supplement that was ever made. My hair was falling out, and the wigs, hats, and scarves were itchy and irritating. I spiked a fever of 106 degrees and was awarded a full week's "vacation" in the hospital to stabilize my body three separate times. It was a war and I felt like the enemy got the best of me more than once.

When you have a high fever, and your immune system

is not working efficiently you get lots of fluids. You also get morphine to manage the pain; those mouth sores were agonizing. And morphine—morphine made me crazy! I am told I attempted to call up my college and change my major; I have no memory of this. I was in a mad as a hatter frenzy dialing the phone, while yelling into the receiver like a desperate addict looking for their next score. I also had dramatic hallucinations, gallons of water pouring out of the hospital sink like a fire hose, filling the room and I was drowning. Perhaps that image came to mind as my lungs had been "floated" with IV fluid—given too much, too soon. I also had a hemorrhage in my left eye, had lost thirty lbs., and in addition to my hair, my eyebrows had begun to fall out. My Dad was my hero at fragile moments. He came in and shaved my head. We knew it was time because I woke up each morning covered in my own hair. His bedside manner with that electric razor was gentle and encouraging. He knew I was delicate, looking in the mirror to see a shadow of a person, defunct of gender, staring back. I did not feel like a woman, just a stick figure and slightly less than human in the grim reflection. It was not necessarily what he said, it was the strength and fearlessness he exhibited by taking on a task that was probably even more difficult for a Dad then it was the patient. I felt so protected in that moment. He and my Mom were there for every unpleasant event and showed a brave face, even though I knew they must have been falling apart on the inside.

My white blood count was very low. I had to get two blood transfusions during my treatments to make my body strong enough to continue. The experience of receiving another person's blood is a miracle, it is also somewhat alarming. My parents were not there as I was given the transfusions at night, and I never felt more alone. I am not going to sugar coat it, watching a stranger's blood enter my veins freaked me out. An unknown person, and alien, someone I knew nothing about was now a part of me. The hospital room was eerily quiet and all I could hear was the solemn hum of the IV. The blood felt warm as it entered my body, and I suddenly felt tingly all over. Without warning a calmness came over me. At that moment, I knew God was holding me. God had a reason and even though I did not understand it, I finally could see the light and had renewed resolve to kick cancer's butt. I recall the realization that this experience had made me resilient. I was enduring things I never thought I would be able to handle. I was no longer a little girl; I was a woman! Even if the reflection said otherwise, I finally believed I would be reborn an even stronger woman because of this experience. If I can handle this, I can handle anything! I also knew, more than ever, that I would never be truly alone again. God would always be with me, in good times and especially the bad ones.

In the first paragraph of this chapter, I told you that I died. No one was there to witness this; however, I believe it happened. The fact of the matter is, I know I was slipping close to the edge of my mortality multiple times in three months. What I want to share with you, my treasured friend, is that many times in life we are given a choice. A choice to stand up and fight or give up and perish. How many times have we heard miraculous stories of car accidents where there was absolutely no hope, and then the injured opens their eyes and takes their first breath after weeks of uncertainty? God gave me a choice: I could allow cancer to take me down or I could take what energy I had left and fight. Fight harder than I ever had or ever would. I remember thinking I would use that last blood transfusion to fuel my body. I would command my mind to seek out better health. Friends, our mind can be our biggest ally or our most ferocious enemy. It all depends on who you are letting in, God or the Devil. The Devil preys on us when he knows we are weak, ready to give up. So, use that last bit of vivacity, no matter how small, to tell the Devil to pack it up and go back to hell as you have more living to do! God is here, you do not need any of that heavy luggage anymore. You do not need to have the perfect words. All you need is a voice and a desire to be in relationship with him. God fixed it and carried me out of the darkness of my nightmare into the light.

All I said to him was, "God please fix this."

*Ally's first performance after
chemotherapy, 1997*

Ally, Elon Graduation, 1998

*   *   *   *

*Use that last bit of vivacity, no matter how
small, to tell the Devil to pack it up and go
back to hell as you have more living to do!*

*   *   *   *

So, guess what? Chemo worked! I finished the three
months of treatment and have been cancer free for over
twenty years now! I returned to college, worked hard and
was able to graduate with my class in three and a half years! I
was able to sing a full hour-long senior recital with Mary Alice playing the harpsichord for the Bach Cantata. I recruited
Jimmy and my opera camp friend, Bryce, to participate in

a couple of duets. My voice had rebounded in prodigious measure and every bit of my three-octave vocal range was unscathed. I was asked to be the vocal soloist for graduation, singing the National Anthem and had plans to attend graduate school (more on this later). I realized that my illness had given me a new lease on life, and I was appreciating all the amazing opportunities coming my way more than I ever had before. I was alive, feeling great, and had been victorious in my war with cancer. I now had perspective, and it was a gift.

The greatest gift: however, I was able to get pregnant on the first try, two times, several years later. I carried both of my miracles without issue to term and delivered two healthy babies naturally. I had a girl and a boy, thirteen months apart, when all of my doctors said I never would. That is God, my friends, he knows our hearts and with him, anything is possible.

Ally, 9 months pregnant, 2004

LIFE LESSON #2
Stay optimistic, do not give up, what does
not kill us makes us stronger.

Cue the Kelly Clarkson song and get your dance on! I just love a happy ending, don't you? It is hard to imagine a happy ending is possible when we are presented with unimaginable obstacles. I started my cancer journey very scared and skeptical. I recall going to the grocery store with my Mom after one of the chemo treatments. I was weak, leaning on the grocery cart, but wanted to attempt to walk around the store with her as that was my only physical activity. We got to the frozen food section and my ears felt like they would explode with loud ringing and my face suddenly became flushed. I was going to faint. My Mom was able to sit me down at the deli so she could finish. I tried to relax and breathe through my body's stampede toward a blackout. I recall shoppers staring at my scarf covered bald head, oversized clothing, and medical mask. In those days you would never see someone in a medical mask in public, unlike today where almost everyone is in a mask, maneuvering the astonishing COVID19 pandemic. I was so tired and frustrated. I was beyond defeated, waking up feeling nauseous every single day, jaded from the intense pain, and stonewalled as I had been robbed of my youthful energy. I was in a very negative place, feeling like an outcast, in a body that was rebelling against every attempt to save it. Morphine's dramatic hallucinogenic trip followed by the forlorn final blood transfusion landed me at rock bottom during that last hospital stay. Rock bottom was a dark, jagged, and dangerous place. The sharp bedrock of my physical demise seemed permanent, and without hope. I did not have the words, but God knew my heart and as the stranger's blood strengthened my feeble body, I felt the switch flip and my once fragile mind had new conviction. I began the first two months of my cancer journey very doubtful and depressed, and for several weeks I rejected calls and visitors. I was in so much pain, was drained from violent daily puking and could not find a happy thought even if it had been tattooed on my arm. I believe God is usually teaching us something or gifting us a skill to use later when we experience affliction. I did not understand the lesson for years and certainly never viewed cancer as a gift at the time. But friends, I did receive an additional gift with my clean bill of health and a new title. I became a keeping the faith, on top of the world, utopian optimist survivor fashioned with rose-colored glasses!

Not long before the end of treatment, I felt the love and support of God and it lit a fire in me. A big, burning flame that churned my rebounding energy into action. I would no longer take feeling good for granted. I would no longer view a delicious meal of real food as commonplace. I would not complain about looking like little orphan Annie—I had hair again for goodness' sake. I was determined to wake up each day and be thankful and appreciate being alive and healthy. All of us will likely experience illness in our lives that will debilitate and piss us off on some level. As I write this, I am obeying the national quarantine for the COVID-19 virus. I would bet that there are thousands of people all over the world feeling resentful and paralyzed either from the virus itself or cabin fever. The point is, we cannot strong arm our way out of a serious illness or situation. We must try to be optimistic as I believe attitude is a make or break regarding the duration of our affliction.

I attended a virtual conference several months ago that was orchestrated by author and motivational speaker, Rachel Hollis. It was eight hours of inspirational magic from great speakers about courage. I learned a new term, "Adversity Quotient," also known as "AQ." AQ, put simply, is turning obstacles into opportunities. Dave Hollis encouraged us all to think carefully about what this epidemic is teaching us. The epidemic is teaching me to appreciate a simpler life and the gift of time. Time to connect with my family without distractions. Time to write a book that I hope will be impactful in the lives of trauma-stricken individuals all over the world. As I write this, I realize that my battle with cancer was a gift. A gift to another person who has been diagnosed and who is frightened of the unknown. Perhaps my obstacle could be an opportunity to show another suffering human that cancer does not have to be a death sentence. My mother-in-law recently battled cancer and underwent chemo. I hated to see her go through it but was glad I was able to hold her hand and say, "I understand what you are going through and am here for you." Sometimes while going through the adversity, we feel completely alone. If I could provide some small level of comfort for others facing what I had conquered, it was definitely worth going through cancer in the first place.

I recently read Psalm 73:26: "My health may fail, and my spirit may grow weak, but God remains the strength of my heart; he is mine forever." I was reincarnated as an eternal optimist thanks to God. The painful experience of cancer made me stronger in mind, body, and spirit. Do not give up. Whatever it is will pass. Though we do not always understand why God gives us hardship, I believe he never gives us anything he believes we cannot overcome.

CHAPTER 3
LAISSEZ LES BONS TEMPS ROULEZ!

It is a new year. The snow is falling, mixed with ice in a winter cocktail that pings the sky light above me, and I cannot get warm. I take another sip of my blackberry sage tea sweetened with local sourwood honey and look to my calendar. January is symbolic for designing a formula for success to guide us in the year ahead; an opportunity to fix the areas of our lives that are not exactly working. For me, those resolutions are tough to nail down as I am held hostage by the same day each year, haunted by a memory that happened over twenty years ago. It is the 21st anniversary of that day and I can still smell the delicate potency of the cigarette you just finished and the pungent taste of it after you kissed me. Today is the day. Today I am letting go of a secret I have kept for twenty-one years. This secret has weighed heavy, like an albatross around my neck, choking the life out of me. This secret has crippled me with shame for two decades even though I was targeted by a predator.

This predator, related to me, abused my trust, and stole my confidence. My naive childhood assumptions served me wrong and revealed a wolf dressed in sheep's clothing. I am unlocking the dungeon, where I have been trapped in my own reoccurring nightmare and saying once and for all, *it was NOT my fault.*

In the spring of my senior year at Elon University I decided to apply for graduate school. I was planning to study opera and began researching schools. I also had the travel bug so exploring new cities was at the top of my list. My forage kept bringing me back to New Orleans, Louisiana. I was drawn to the French influence, Cajun food, warm climate and of course, the music. It did not take long for me to sign up for the next opera audition date at Loyola University and book my flight. Have you ever embarked on a new adventure and all the pieces align like a jigsaw puzzle, giving you a small nudge to jump right in? I found a direct flight, at a last-minute discount, that allowed me to fly in and out of New Orleans and back to Raleigh the same day.

I caught the early morning plane, landed in New Orleans, and was in a cab on my way to audition at Loyola University twenty minutes later. Loyola, located in the Garden District of New Orleans, is a quick streetcar ride from Bourbon Street and only 25 minutes from the Louis Armstrong New Orleans International Airport. I was captivated by the gorgeous French Colonial architecture adorned with colorful flowers on cast iron balconies that skirted the streetcar line. I stopped at a local dive and tried my first fried oyster po' boy and a glass of sweet tea. I felt a connection to the Garden District of New Orleans immediately and it seemed as though my pulse was beating in rhythm with the jazz musician playing nearby.

I arrived at Loyola at 1pm, brushed my teeth, curled my hair, and freshened up my makeup. I wore a bright red fit and flair dress with a modest neckline that tied at the waist and fell below my knee. I applied matching red lipstick and took one last look in the mirror, uttering a quiet prayer that I would come across as confident and unforgettable, knowing the panel had a long list of applicants that day. My hair was still short, but I was looking more like Lucille Ball instead of little orphan Annie. Although I still did not quite look like myself, I was thankful for how quickly my voice rebounded after being dormant for months. I decided to kick off the audition with Leonard Bernstein's "Glitter and Be Gay" from *Candide* as it would show my vocal range and acting ability. The panel of judges was made up of three highly respected music department professionals. A husband-and-wife duo who were both opera instructors and performers and the Dean of Music. I loved this aria; it was fun to sing and as I took my preparatory breath, I felt a warm glow come over my body. It had only been a few months since I had completed chemotherapy treatment and yet I was singing the hardest song regarding stamina and range that I had ever learned. God had given me my health back and I leaned into every moment of that audition with intense gratitude. I was proud to share the gift I was still able to use after cancer had invaded the space only centimeters from where my voice lived.

I guess I did okay as the judges offered me a place in the Loyola Opera Program on the spot! Not only did I get in, but I was also awarded a 90% scholarship to attend. After receiving the offer, I was invited to sit in on a music history class before leaving to catch my plane. In the class I met Charissa, an outgoing, kind and immediately likable music therapy major. We hit it off instantly and when she learned I would be moving to New Orleans in the fall she asked me if I had a place to live. Charissa and two other sophomores had signed a lease on a four-bedroom apartment only a couple of blocks from Loyola. After the class was over, I met Dana and Jen. They were just as welcoming as Charissa, and the conversation proceeded as if we had known each other for years. Within thirty minutes the three undergrads enthusiastically requested I be their fourth roommate, and without a second thought I said yes!

I boarded the plane to return to Elon and could not wipe the silly grin off my face. How had my next several years been decided, planned, and funded in a matter of a few hours? I was dumbfounded, and ecstatically grateful. I felt like someone had turned on a light inside of me, and I was finally living. I reverted to my childhood self when I returned home for treatment. I had missed out on a whole list of "firsts" in college while I was sick. It was almost as if God was gifting me a second chance to have a more traditional collegiate experience without the extended break. I was a homebody at heart, but the almost thirteen-hour drive from my home in Virginia to New Orleans did not divert me one bit. I was given a second chance at life, and I was determined to take it!

Charissa, Dana, Jen and I moved into a second story apartment in a 1940s Créole style house two weeks before classes began in August. The layout of the kitchen and family room was an open concept, with a gorgeous vintage metal ceiling and large picture windows that overlooked a lush courtyard which had been nourished by the constant humidity in the air. It was in that kitchen I became a foodie, creating art with fresh ingredients and herbs, paired with budget friendly red wines, all while Sting's sultry voice filled the space between the four of us. We were lucky to see Sting perform at the Saenger Theatre in New Orleans that fall. Lucky because it was a small venue, and we barely had enough money for the tickets as we were all on student budgets. Music was more important than eating at that point so pasta would be a staple for a few weeks.

Sting introduced an eclectic new album and delighted us with a combination of genres including rock, new wave, jazz, and world music. I remember closing my eyes and feeling seduced by the velvet timbre of his voice as it spun around me. Sting was an open book that night, sharing with the intimate audience his devotion to tantric yoga and how it had impacted his sensual life with his wife. I had always thought of myself as an open book, valuing the honesty of being who I was good or bad. Sting's commitment to passion and honesty in his performance that night left a gentle footprint on my soul. I took in the beautiful lyrics of

"When We Dance" thinking briefly about losing Eric and battling cancer and without warning my brain was flooded with the image of falling in love. I was falling in love with my city, and it was a love affair that I hoped would never end. I felt like a different person, the person God wanted me to be, living a passionate and rich life with a deeply contented heart.

I had fallen hard for New Orleans. I loved the food, eating decadent beignets sprinkled with powdered sugar at Café de Monde, spicy jambalaya and drinking red sangria at the Gumbo Shop, devouring steamed crawfish dripping in butter at Jacques-Imo's and delicious homemade pralines in Jackson Square. I loved the culture and traditions. I attended a Mardi Gras ball in a sapphire satin, off the shoulder gown with feather trim with a group of my church friends. I caught beads and cheered for locals on colorful floats as my friends and I swayed to zydeco music while sipping frozen daiquiris. I sang opera in stunning theaters to standing room only crowds. I even loved my work!

Most of us musicians must work multiple jobs to make ends meet. Some of those jobs are not music related. My primary job was as a salesperson at a fancy bridal shop, and I had a church job for extra cash. I was able to invest in gorgeous, unique clothing with my discount and hefty commission checks. This was the first time I was paid to work in a career that fed one of my first passions, fashion! I had entered year seven of my obsession with fashion and my unique style was beginning to take shape. I guess you could say I was the product of Kate Spade and Alexander McQueen if they had a baby at Anthropologie. Highbrow, edgy, minimalistic, sometimes bohemian and fun! To this day I still love mixing patterns and am drawn to lush fabrics and beaded embellishments. I was courageous with my outfit choices and did not care what anyone had to say about my bold fashion decisions during that season in my life.

Finally, I had fallen in love with the people. Never in my life had I enjoyed such a diverse group of friends, all in different circles, providing invites to the best locales in New

Orleans. Dancing and laughing the night away without a care in the world. One night I was sitting on the expansive porch at the Columns Hotel enjoying a French martini with friends and I took a long, satisfying breath. I replayed my first year in my new home. All my passions were being fed and I had finally arrived at the life I had always dreamed of and was showing up as the best possible version of myself. It was another gift from God, and I was eternally thankful.

My second year of graduate school started with a move to a one-bedroom apartment near Touro Hospital, slightly farther from campus but still in the Garden District. I decided to move out on my own as I could not imagine leaving New Orleans anytime soon and Dana and Charissa would soon be moving to Los Angeles. The new apartment was a three story walk up with a pool and motorized security gate that led you into a private parking lot. Having a parking lot and a pool was unheard of in NOLA as was the rent—I only paid three hundred dollars a month for my own place! As the first week rounded to a close, I sat out on the stoop admiring the canopy of elegant white magnolias strung together by emerald satin leaves that draped the brick wall surrounding the property. It was August and the intense heat and dewy humidity layered the air and soaked my clothes, hair, and face. There was no point to investing money or time into make-up during the NOLA summer as it would inevitably run down your face.

My salty gaze was interrupted by a chatty group of tourists following a guide toward Lafayette Cemetery No. 1, located a couple of blocks away. I thought back to when I first toured the new apartment; two blocks away a boisterous funeral parade was making its way to the Lafayette Cemetery No. 1 that day. I loved the idea that the deceased was being celebrated in the walk to their final resting place. The trumpet led the band, accompanied by saxophone, trombone, tuba, and snare drum. I began humming along with the procession of loved ones as they sang "When the Saints Go Marching In." I was entranced by the very special New Orleans funeral tradition, realizing it was a gift to be a witness that day. There are so many ways to translate death and up until that moment, my only experience was a traditional funeral. I had only attended three funerals in my life, and they were very somber events, the music, eulogy, and scripture almost made my heart hurt worse. The funeral parade was my first encounter with the idea that celebrating the life of the deceased is also a very acceptable way to say goodbye and begin to process grief. I vowed to myself then and there that when God decided it was time for me to pass on, I would leave behind plans for an epic celebration. A celebration with champagne and glitter, on my favorite beach, my children, and grandchildren dancing, singing, and laughing while sharing treasured family memories. I imagined what the makeshift instruments and hand maid crowns would look like on curly haired grandsons and daughters. I could almost make out their precious faces in my wild daydream and then my phone rang.

I answered the phone, and my parents were on the other end. I assumed they had called to check on my progress with unpacking but there was another purpose to the call. One of my cousins, Stan, was traveling to New Orleans in a couple of months and they asked I put him up on my pull-out cot, located in my family room. He was traveling to New Orleans to see a sporting event and invited me to attend with him. I had been around this first cousin more than a dozen times since I was a small child, so I knew him relatively well. He always came over and talked to Kiki and me during family events when other relatives were only talking to the adults. He was the fun Uncle so to speak; approachable, funny, and marginally cool from what I could tell. Stan had a way about him that immediately made you feel safe, and our family all assumed he was gay as he had never married. Our family has always been very private so Stan's romantic status would never be spoken of and well you know what happens when you make assumptions…

Stan called the week before he planned to travel to New Orleans to give me the flight details so I could pick him up. I was a little nervous as I was not sure how to entertain a man twenty-five years my senior in a town I was still learning myself. The day Stan arrived was slightly rainy but by the time we got to my apartment from the airport, the rain had stopped. Stan had never been to New Orleans so we decided to walk around so he could experience the ornate landscape of the Garden District and we would eventually find a restaurant for dinner when we were hungry. The conversation flowed like a calming river, and I immediately felt comfortable. He took long drags of a cigarette as we walked and talked about my graduate program. He revealed very little about himself in our conversation, focusing on the details of my life in New Orleans. He listened with intense fascination, using the attention to bait me like a mixed-up fish. Once he extinguished the cigarette, he gently took my hand in his without a word. We walked hand in hand for several blocks and it did not occur to me to be uncomfortable, seeing as my childhood hunch held firm that he was gay. In addition, our family rituals were deeply Southern and unapologetically affectionate. Long lingering hugs, hand holding and terms of endearment like "Sugar" and "Darling" were a distinct part of our family culture. It always seemed wholesome but then again, I am recalling adult behavior from when I was a child. In that moment I was caught in a confusing web between childhood and adult independence after requiring constant emotional and physical care during my battle with cancer. Stan's outward character boasted confidence and when he touched my hand, it still felt familial, and safe. He had broken the touch barrier and blurred the lines of our relationship; I was utterly mystified but, in that moment, I still trusted him.

We ducked into a local bistro for dinner as the sky threatened another rain shower. I ordered a glass of wine and tried to relax. I am a people pleaser and often put pressure on myself to be the perfect hostess. I was out of practice as I did not entertain much in college and not at all after my battle with cancer. My parents were expert party planners and fun administrators, hosting an epic Christmas Eve party for their friends for decades. It came easy for them, and they were good at it. I wished comfort with entertaining were genetic or even intuitive, but truth be told, I never felt truly comfortable as a mistress of ceremonies at that time.

I do not remember what either of us ordered that night. I do remember thinking it odd that he did not ask me about my recent battle with cancer. I had just hit the eighteen-month anniversary of being cancer free and thought he might wish me congratulations. I had also just had my port-a-cath removed as cancer had stayed away for over a year and the remission seemed permanent. I looked at Stan like a father figure initially because of our age difference and he seemed worldly and wise. I was still struggling to see myself as a woman after cancer required me to rely on my family for every physical and emotional need.

We returned to the apartment around eight p.m. after dinner. As I turned around after locking the door, Stan was staring at me. His cunning blue eyes, an ocular device, searching my unsuspecting hazel eyes for opportunity. The vibe between us had changed and I was uneasy. Stan started to speak and then stopped himself before the words escaped his lips. I asked him what he wanted to say. "Can I ask you a weird question?" he continued. I nodded. "May I brush your hair?" he asked with slight trepidation. My mind was reeling. Why would he want to brush my hair? Was this the point in the evening where I pop popcorn, put on "Sex and the City" and we gab like a couple of gal pals? I was so confused, but it seemed harmless enough, so I said, "Okay." I went to the bathroom to get my brush and tried very hard to command my mind to believe it was not a bad idea.

My post cancer hair had finally grown long enough to allow for a short ponytail. I was born with relatively straight strawberry blonde hair, but my hair grew back in more auburn with tight curls that loosened over time and length. When I came back into the family room, Stan was sitting on the pull-out cot. He took the flat backed brush from my shaky hand and motioned for me to sit down in front of him. He began brushing my fresh curls gently, without a word. It felt nice to have someone brush my hair and I convinced myself that he was just trying to be kind to a girl who had just been through hell with her battle with cancer. A girl who finally had hair again. I could not have been more wrong. Stan paused after five minutes of brushing my hair and more questions followed. The next two questions and the actions that resulted, changed everything I believed about myself. Suddenly I found myself walking toward a dungeon of shame, hand in hand with the Devil, a seemingly easy departure from my Christian values.

"May I kiss you, Allison?"

"May I take you to the bedroom, Allison?"

I had just turned twenty-three years old, was still a virgin and I had no idea how to handle myself confidently with a man old enough to be my father. And let us not forget, he was in MY FAMILY! I was also afraid of what would happen if I said no. He led me to the bedroom, no more questions were asked, he just proceeded with an agenda he had clearly been planning all night. He asked me to put on lingerie, which I did not own, so I put on my pajamas. Then he asked me to take them off, not able to comprehend why I did not own lingerie. The pajamas I chose were one of the four sets my Mom bought me during chemo. I squeezed my eyes tight, feeling as though I was light years away from the safety net of my family unit. Those lovely, emerald green satin pajamas with the four covered buttons that allowed easy access to the port-a-cath were now providing easy passage for an indecent fling that would haunt me for decades.

My snafued scar from the removal of the port-a-cath was still fresh below my collarbone. I could not imagine how anyone would find me desirable as there were still visible traces that I had been a severely ill cancer patient with several highly visible scars to prove it. He laid me on the bed and removed his own clothes revealing his erection. He was proud of his penis, and I got the feeling it was not always ready to stand at attention. He joined me on the bed and began tracing the freckles that covered the mountains and valleys of my body with his fingers. He marked me with a wet kiss on my trembling lips, his tongue invading my delicate mouth with rabid ecstasy. The tainted kiss quickly wandered to the unchartered skin on my neck, chest, and breasts. His Jekyll and Hyde two-faced charm had me perplexed, exposing a lover and a beast in each deliberate blink of my eyes. He explored my secret lady garden, touching me harder and faster and I hated myself for reacting to it. I had never been that naked or vulnerable before; my body shaking like a Caribbean maraca and my heart beating like a Yamani cymbal playing monkey on steroids. My mind was on fire and I felt the Devil pulling me into the seventh circle of hell while my body convulsed by the scandalous erotic play. Stan then instructed me to touch his prick until he got off. I felt like a gullible student and him the disgraceful teacher who thought he had a right to inflict his sick sexual lesson on me. He rolled over and immediately fell asleep the moment he got what he wanted. The acrimony of the despicable act that had just occurred in my virginal bed began a slow burn on me and suddenly I understood the meaning of bitter.

I laid there all night, devastated, feeling dirty and violated. I was convinced I had been a casualty of a curse, spurred on by an enemy who had charmed the dark arts against me. My mind accepted all possibilities, including voodoo dolls and witchcraft. I still had my virginity, but Stan's sly wizardry had robbed me of my innocence. He stole a moment of intimacy from me while his evil charm escorted me to shameful pre-marital foreplay that should have been a gift to my husband. I was so furious with myself for allowing him to touch me in such a deplorable way but felt helpless, my voice rendered mute. He was the worst kind of monster, deceiving my trust, slaughtering my self-love, and forever altering my vision for my marital future in a matter of minutes. Sexual exploitation appeared to be a hobby for Stan, and he knew how to rope me into the humiliating endeavor with his toolbox of trickery. I felt attacked and disarmed. His carnal action was premeditated and the forcefulness of his words and touch made me feel like a helpless and endangered pawn.

I looked over to see my Valerie Fleming photograph of an angel, overcome by hardship, doubled over a tomb, sobbing without reprieve. Her once vibrant wings now lay fractured while her shimmering eyes burned hot from the stigma, she could not unsee. I could almost see my own guardian angel breaking into a million pieces like this picture of the vulnerable statue. The thief, that now snored in my corrupted bed, had fooled me. He had never been married and his confusing metrosexual approach to life, his refined mannerisms, and liberal politics had left me bamboozled. Why did I allow myself to assume he was gay? Stan's intoxicating beguilement and a couple glasses of wine had duped me into a decision that inevitably made me hate myself for twenty years. He knew a couple glasses of wine would relax me and brushing my hair would potentially arouse me. Stan also knew I was too naïve to realize that brushing my hair could cause such a result. Stan's crafty manipulation was well-practiced, and he had mastered every nuance of the forbidden relationship.

My sisters, allow me to share that those forbidden relationships only exist in secret, behind closed curtains, and attract the worse kind of human, an impotent snake with a decaying soul. The impostor who is attempting to sell you on the highly classified affair has countless skeletons in his closet, badges of honor for the selfish control he has inflicted on a myriad of women. Do not allow yourself to believe the poetry of promises that escape his lying lips, there is only one goal here and it has nothing to do with the fantasy you are carefully contemplating in your misled mind. It is all about domination and the wickedness that pours so freely from him is camouflaged as the most intriguing aphrodisiac. His slippery love potion, however, will surely leave you poisoned, suffering the illicit love transaction that should never have been entertained. I have wished for a do over hundreds of times but the reenactment I pray for now, is the one where you, my friend, run like hell before this happens to you.

My sentimentality of all those family reunions felt like a lie and I wondered what his respectable parents would think of his abusive treatment of me. I also wondered what my own parents would say if they ever saw him again. I have lived two decades in denial, mis-labeling and minimizing what Stan did to me as a coping mechanism. He knew what he was doing and that the paralyzing fear of shame would keep me quiet. I was no longer an open book; I was a changed woman who had guarded secrets she was keeping. I was also a woman who deeply cared what others thought of her, fearing judgement would find me around every corner. Stan tried to sell me on the idea that what was happening between us was beyond our control. He declared that we had fallen in love. I allowed myself to believe he loved me for longer than I would like to admit, unable to process that he was a predator. He even admitted to me that I was not the first family member he had attempted to seduce. I felt sick and deeply sad. I also felt slightly relieved that this had happened to me and not my younger sister, Kiki.

The emotional attachment I experienced with Stan made me feel ashamed and insane. I was desperate to regulate the quickly sinking ship of my mind, mistaking my almost drowning in abuse for love. Why did I think I had fallen for him? How did a very obvious morally and ethically wrong entrapment fool me? My runaway mind became a roller coaster wishing I were a character in *Gone With the Wind* where it was acceptable to love your cousin. Maybe if I could make myself believe that we were in love, I could somehow rectify my hate for myself. I was disoriented mentally, drastically so, like I had endured a dramatic brain injury. How had I allowed this to happen? Was I not stronger and smarter than this? I was a cancer survivor warrior for Christ's sake, why did I not use my voice?

It has taken me twenty years to work through the details of this. I blamed myself for years, combing through every moment of the visit and how I had sent him signals that I did not intend to send. The fact of the matter is I was inexperienced, and I trusted that this member of my family had my best interests at heart. I also allowed myself to be in a situation in my one-bedroom apartment that I had no idea how to get out of. Stan took advantage of the setting and my sexual immaturity to lead me down a road I would never have traveled if I had been in my right mind. My body was not the only part of me he violated, he did a number on my mind. My mind was irrevocably botched, so much so that I allowed myself to settle for my first husband, believing I did not deserve true love. I was a dirty girl who hooked up with a cousin, might as well settle for a man who was willing to marry me. I felt as though I had been branded like a cult member and worried, I would be judged for the mistake, so I stayed quiet.

I hated the secret I was harboring; I could not even look at myself in the mirror, and the depression I felt spiraled me down a dangerous path. I started going to bars, alone. I started to drink, a lot. One night I got drunk, very drunk, and I had no money for a cab. I began staggering the two miles home. Those two miles had good blocks and bad blocks, the bad littered with would be criminals contemplating robberies or rape. I knew better but I was reckless, how could it possibly get worse? God sent me a guardian angel that night. A cab driver, and Good Samaritan, picked me up ten minutes later and took me home. He did not care I had no money; he did not want to see something bad happen to me. My conversation with Johnny-on-the-spot that night was an important intervention from God. He had seen what happens on the "bad blocks" and his horrific recount of late-night crimes made me want to get sober immediately. He gave me a reassuring smile and promised that whatever I was going through would get better but, in the meantime, I needed to make better decisions.

I thanked my Guardian Angel for his chivalry and exited the cab with a bang. My bumbling farewell and swift head collision on the cab's door jamb produced an almost immediate hangover headache. I struggled to find my footing on the curb after my clumsy crash, realizing the affects of my reckless alcohol binge were still coming to light. I stumbled up two flights of steps into my apartment and collapsed in the bathroom. I was sick all night. Fresh tears cascaded from my eyes like an angry storm for hours, leaving behind a slapdash trail of mascara that camouflaged the numerous freckles on my cheeks. My mind was flooded with questions. How am I ever going to survive this? How am I ever going to be able to look in the mirror again? Why didn't I say no? Why did he think he could do this to me? The days, weeks, and months that followed were impossibly hard. The colors had faded in my beautiful pictorial canvas of New Orleans and there were painful reminders everywhere of my horror filled visit with Stan. My love affair with the "Paris of the South" was over and the beloved image was permanently vandalized. I could not imagine a scenario where I could heal from what happened while living in that apartment. That apartment, my own personal hell, that reminded me of my abomination every single day. There was only one thing I could think of to do, leave.

I graduated in May and immediately moved to Washington, D.C. I could not continue to live in a city with so many triggers of the abuse I had endured. Looking back on that decision now, I feel intense regret. How did I allow Stan to ruin my stunning and deeply tender relationship with New Orleans? How did I allow him to rob me of precious time in a place that invigorated my soul and delighted my senses the year before? I could not process what had happened to me and my solution was to run from it. I would start over and no one would ever have to know. The problem with that choice is that inevitably the trauma resurfaces. If you do not deal with the trauma, and work through all parts of the grief, you remain unprotected from future violations. I should have seen a therapist; I should have allowed a professional to explain that it was not my fault. Instead, I chose to run to a new town where no one knew me and start over as if nothing had happened. Two years later, I was raped, while sleeping, in Arlington, Virginia. Trauma had found me again, and it was so much worse.

Ally, Mardi Gras Ball, 1999

Ally, Loyola Graduation, 2000

LIFE LESSON #3
Translate the truth in the trauma to allow transformation.

January 2000 was the moment I became traumaniacal, and the day after Stan left, I discovered a permanent crack in my foundation. The crack in my moral and mental foundation, inflicted by the evil doer had permanently damaged my self-esteem and my personal view of myself was one of hate. The chink in my moral and mental armor also meant that I was an easy target and the hate I felt for myself eventually eliminated my desire to hope for anything good in the present or future. I had also stopped praying and had no relationship with God, feeling as though I had passed the point of no return and permanently failed him. I had already been wounded by trauma when Eric was killed by a drunk driver and shortly after I battled a highly aggressive form of cancer. But nothing, I mean nothing, no trauma I have ever experienced, has haunted me the way the incestuous abuse has.

I could not run to escape; I could not make the images cease that continued to flood my brain as I tried to sleep. I was being preyed upon even when I was awake, my unstable mind had become my adversary. Imagine all the casual, harmless jokes made by others over the years about "kissing cousins" and such, and my constant battle to choke down the red telling blush of embarrassment. Imagine the shame I carried deep within me for decades and the fear of anyone knowing that I had kissed my cousin, and so much more. Being haunted all the time meant that the dungeon that housed my incestuous abuse was getting smaller and I felt the pressure building as if an explosion was imminent. The fire for my blow up was being fueled by men who aspired to control me. It was not just Stan. It was the entitled New Yorker I met at college, the arrogant Greek Chef I met in Greensboro and the Hispanic Doctor I met in Chicago who all tried to steal intimacy from me. Intimacy that was safeguarded, like a treasure. I managed to escape each of those additional three attacks with a good swift knee to the groin. But I was still the picture of madness for years and felt as though I had a sign pinned on my shirt that read, "Please use me for your selfish evil."

Many years after leaving NOLA I made the mistake of reaching back out to Stan to try to understand why it had all happened. My foundation remained splintered from the unresolved trauma and I hoped a conversation with him would somehow set me free. I was extremely vulnerable, picking up the pieces of another failed relationship and he knew exactly where to sneak his way back into a forbidden pursuit with me. I cannot even tell you the details of how it happened because I have blocked it from my memory. It goes back to that old saying, "fool me once, shame on you...but fool me twice, shame on me!" How had I allowed this to happen to me a second time? Shame was my permanent accessory, my constant for twenty years, TWENTY YEARS! Please learn from my journey, ladies, reaching back out to the predator to attempt to make sense of what happened will only leave you worse for wear. The predator is going to continue to try to abuse the situation and cannot be part of the solution. Being in touch with the villain of your past gives him power and fuels his ego. We are not meant to understand the inner workings of a predator's mind nor would we want to. Do yourself a favor and cut him off and do the work! I am thankful for the #metoo movement for giving me the courage to speak out so that other women (and my six daughters) would hear these stories and hopefully assimilate the behavior of a predator before becoming their victim.

Love always felt conditional to me during that season of my life. Men wanted sex, and they were willing to take it at any cost. It did not matter my morals or boundaries. It did not matter if I said, "No." There was always more to the very unhealthy one-sided conversation they would attempt to angle in their favor. The ending was always the same, I was alone and wounded. Have you ever been a victim of conditional love where love had to be earned? What terms were established for you to experience that "love" which was not really love at all? What happens to conditional love when times get tough? Does conditional love endure or does your significant other cut and run when things get real? Being lonely sucks, believe me I know. I have been there, many times. But what is worse, living a lie so you are not alone? Sharing your life with a selfish jerk who is using you? Living your truth is brave but certainly not easy. What does that even mean, "living your truth"? In my humble opinion "living your truth" means you deserve more than the small piece of affection they are offering. It means you are not having to numb your daily existence with drugs or alcohol to get through the bad parts. It means you are not waking each day, convincing yourself, over and over again, that the lie is ok. It is not ok, and you should demand more. You deserve to bask in the joy that thrives from living a deeply soulful life. Does conditional love feel soulful? NO! It sounds soul crushing if you ask me.

In order for me to completely live my truth, I had to evaluate the lies I was telling myself. My goal is to help others so allow me to share the vile lies I wore like a suit full of hate for decades.

The Lies...
I am a jezebel.
I am a horrible person.
I am no longer loved by God.
Everyone is going to judge me.
My family is going to blame me.
I do not deserve to be loved.

I had to face what happened to me once and for all, dispel the lies, and ask God to help me. I did not know what to say or where to start. I simply asked him to show me the light and bit by bit I was able to chip away at the many years of lies, shame, regret, and depression that kept me in complete darkness. I was spinning out of control in a tornado of adversity and the prolonged exposure to all the horrific events was eventually going to kill me. Two decades of sweeping my chronic trauma under the rug had become a pattern. I had to break that pattern, find my truth, and jump into action so on that cursed twenty first anniversary here is what I did…

I prayed. The praying was not always pretty, sometimes I yelled and cursed the Devil. God was the only one who could heal the big load of baggage I was carrying so I started talking to him every day. It took time and scripture study, but I finally realized and believed wholeheartedly that I am forever loved by the Lord.

I shared all of it, every ugly detail of the trauma with my husband, Kevin. I had to create that line of trust with my person, and you know what? Kevin held and cried with me. He dried my tears and kissed my cheeks. He loved me and cherished me in a way I never believed was possible after the incestuous abuse. He did not cast judgement on me even though it took me almost ten years to share this embarrassing part of my history with him. The fact of the matter is, most of us have regrets and shame but that does not mean we are not worthy of love in its purest form with our perfect person.

I wrote down what happened to me so I could purge it from my soul. I had to find resolution in the pages and banish all the lies I was telling myself. It took me twenty-one years to write it down, but I finally feel free. I also feel like a bad ass, having finally harnessed the courage to tell my story out loud, and proud. I pray daily that my truth and courage will save another woman's life, or her fragile soul.

I identified the cursed anniversary with new traditions, positive activities that would eclipse the memories that have clouded that day. Put your foot down and do not allow the calendar to have power over you any longer. I was lucky, God blessed me here with a gift that allowed me to reclassify that horrid day and the coincidence is astounding. My sweet husband Kevin's birthday is the same day of the year as that sexual trauma. That is another heavenly sign from God, my friends, and when we began to celebrate Kevin each year, the cursed memory of that day began to die. Focusing on the very magical gift of Kevin's birth to my life allowed me to close the door on all the baggage that I carried from that once foredoomed day. It was clear, that was another cue from God that it was time to be brave, deal with the trauma, and move on with the beautiful life I was creating with Kevin and our seven children. The other message I was receiving from God was that my moral and mental foundation had finally been restored and I could begin to love myself the way God loves me.

Choosing to stare trauma square in the face is scary but facing it is the first step to healing. I believe in you, my courageous friend, imagine what freedom from your past would mean for your future! Imagine how your family will be blessed by your healing, seeing the beautiful person you are who is no longer controlled by the nightmare. You have been distracted for years, losing precious quality time with your loved ones. You can cast out those demons and start fresh! What are some ways you could reclassify a memory that is haunting your calendar year after year? What are some steps you could take to redirect your focus to positivity? Open your eyes and appreciate all the good things God has provided for your life. Investigate what living a deeply soulful life means for you and make room for the love you are so deserving of, whenever it makes its presence known.

Living with regret is heavy and I could not bring myself to go back to New Orleans until recently. My city, like me, was changed, beaten, and broken from Hurricane Katrina. Most of my friends had relocated and I felt like a stranger in the city that I used to call home. I walked the Garden District ghost tour with my husband and our college bound daughter taking in the spicy aroma of Cajun food and the distant chiming of the streetcar at each stop. We chatted with a local about the ghost sightings in his home over the years and my daughter's face awoke with discovery and passion, bringing the legends from years of TV shows and books to life for her. I was reminded of my pre-abuse twenty-two-year-old self, in my innocent daughter that day and the reunion with NOLA brimmed with hope and recovery. I was saved by my mighty rebirth, a miraculous gift, and I no longer felt ashamed. Doing the therapeutic work of recovering from incestuous abuse at home in Virginia was important to my process but the true test of recovery for me was returning to the unsanctified setting of the exploitation.

For years I visualized a return to New Orleans like sitting in the middle of the eye of a storm. The haunting memories rigorous like savage debris during Hurricane Katrina. No shelter was strong enough to withstand the ferocious current of flooded memories so I remained a refugee, estranged from the place I once loved. But I had outsmarted the Devil, I resolved the lies, I was armed with truth, and that truth had set me free. The forgotten colors from my love affair with New Orleans came alive once again and my faith that I once thought was dead, had been restored. I had been healed and reborn after trauma; I finally observed New Orleans the way I did at our conception and a wiser woman stood where that impulsive collegiate had devoured that delicious oyster po' boy more than twenty years earlier. I had been given a second chance to love a place that had left deep scars and the gift of wisdom to understand the lesson. I whispered thank you to God and realized that I was finally going to be able to have a relationship with NOLA again. I had been freed from my dark confinement of shame. I had fresh eyes, a healthy outlook and peace from the nightmare that haunted me repeatedly for twenty years. I can finally say it is over, it was not my fault, and I am free. I also have the genuine love of a man who rescued me from the prison of my past. A man who knows all my secrets and continues to love me unconditionally.

One verse that really helped me to visualize being saved by God from the darkness of that hideous dungeon was Psalm 107: 13-16.

Psalm 107: 13-16

"Then they cried to the Lord in their trouble, and he delivered them from their distress. He brought them out of darkness and the shadow of death and burst their bonds apart. Let them thank the Lord for his steadfast love, for his wondrous works to the children of man! For he shatters the doors of bronze and cuts in two the bars of iron."

CHAPTER 4
THE CLOWN
PARADE

The blue haired, white faced polka dot covered clown ushered us to our seats. The three-ring circus pavilion was still dark, my eyes soon adjusted to see multi-colored clowns in the four corners of the massive space. I found myself wondering about the people behind the kaleidoscopic masks. My childhood church adopted a clown ministry and I had been a clown a handful of times myself. For a quiet, introverted girl, it was an opportunity to try out a more assertive persona safely and anonymously, without criticism. Becoming a black and white mime clown one Sunday a year is prismatic whimsy but, why would an adult choose a profession that allows them to be anonymous every single day? My thoughts were interrupted as the house lights came on, revealing acrobats, more clowns, and the ring master in the distance. As the lion & tiger show began, seven sets of eyes came alive, reflecting wonder and magic. The sight of my children, experiencing pure amazement and outlandish discovery at the circus, a landmark childhood event, was a moment I wish I could have frozen in time. I envied them the unsullied view that was pure as the driven snow and silently prayed that each of my precious angels would always remember those virtuous childhood events. My mind also drifted to consider the many coming of age lessons I had yet to teach, and I prayed they would all avoid the peril I had endured. I believe most parents hope their children will look back upon their childhood with the happiest of memories. I certainly want the loop that plays in their memory to be a happy one; however, more than that I hope we told them enough how extraordinary, smart, and capable they are to do anything they choose to pursue. And with regards to love and who they choose to spend their lives with, I hope we said "I love you" enough and imparted the wisdom that they never have to settle because they deserve to find their perfect match.

God has blessed me with a blended family of seven children. Six of the seven children are girls. Speaking of relating to a tiger, it is one thing to break my heart but hurt my kids and Mama is going to pounce! My desire to write this book stemmed from a long night of tears after one of my teenagers had her heart broken for the first time. I realized that my life lessons could likely help my sweet kiddos and hopefully other folks' kiddos too. That night I tried to explain to my daughter that dating can feel like a parade of clowns also known as jerks and the experience a sick joke.

I also believe there is a lot to learn from the people we date. Our dating life teaches us about ourselves, what we are looking for in another person, what kind of personality is a good match, common interests that are shared, core values and so much more. We must use careful discernment to decipher deal breakers and compromises in our relationships and what constitutes pulling the plug or getting more serious. I have a lot of experience in this arena, and feel it is time to pull back the curtain and reveal the wisdom under the big top.

When you grow up with a Dad who is a gynecologist, dating can be challenging at times. One example that comes to mind is my Dad emerging from the back yard complete with a very loud chain saw on its highest setting when asked to meet one of my boyfriends for the first time. I seem to recall he even revved the engine a couple of times before making eye contact with my beau. Yea, that happened. Let us also not forget that I learned about the birds and the bees at age five and by the time I was in middle school I was well versed in all the very scary, disgusting, life destroying diseases you could catch from unprotected sex. I had a firm moral foundation thanks to my parents and my church and all the horror stories of what could happen if you chose to play Russian Roulette with sex was enough to keep me in line. Being choosy about who we date can be lonely at times, but I was determined to choose men with honorable character and emotional depth, not sexual charisma.

I am going to be real with you, friend, parenting teenagers in the current social media driven world is rough. Any attempt to share moral guidance and lessons from our generation's experiences is quickly tuned out by the Airpods that are now a permanent accessory. Forget about building a virtual safety net. You can lock down that device with parental apps and screen time perimeters, but they still find a way. And they are way smarter than I ever was at that age. The opinion of their peers is everything to my teenage girls and those peers can be downright mean. Picture the pompous character Regina George in *Mean Girls* times one thousand. Keep the tissues handy, their favorite snack foods in the pantry, an open mind and get ready to listen. When they want to talk to us it is the greatest gift, Mama, but you must listen without judgement and please do not ever make them feel ashamed for mistakes that have already been made. Look for teaching moments when you can but without coming on too strong. Mental health is very fragile, and kids have more pressure than we ever did. High school now feels like college and middle school like high school. Kids cannot even be kids the way we could because the expectations start earlier and earlier. Education has become a competition instead of a tool to develop a lifelong love of learning.

Speaking of tools…it really is funny, or tragically sad, how many bad first dates I have had over the course of my life. I have dated the guys that used to date guys. I have dated the guys who liked me because I have big boobs and decided that red hair equals a "slam dunk" in the bedroom. I have dated drug addicts and alcoholics. I have dated the guys who forgot to tell me they were married. I have dated control freaks. I have dated the ones that are incapable of commitment. I have dated the Casanovas that have had more action than Hugh Heffner. It feels like I have dated them all. At one point in my twenties, I decided to characterize the exes as clowns.

Did you know there are about a hundred different varieties of clowns? There are roughly ten main categories and then anywhere from ten to fifty specific clowns in the sub-categories under the initial ten. That is a lot of face paint! We are all familiar with "Ronald," the harmless face of McDonald's but let us face it, most of the clowns we, or at least I, think of are creepy, crazy, or monstrous. Thanks to Stephen King and director, Andrés Muschietti, we have a new terrifying image with which to associate the lunatic clown also known as Pennywise from *IT*. What a scary dude he is, makes me never want to go to the circus ever again! Todd Phillips also painted a masterful interpretation of what I like to call the crazy clown with the adaptation of *The Joker* where we see how past trauma can leave a once innocent man unhinged.

The astonishing thing I realized recently: I have been acting like a clown most of my life. I may not be wearing face paint or juggling bowling pins; however, I felt nameless in my own skin. I portrayed myself as the mime clown from my youth, as a vanilla face in a crowd with nothing interesting to share, desperately burying my undercover past deeper and deeper. I wanted to seem boring, it was safer than damaged. The secret of my incest altered the very fiber of my being, and nothing was good enough and I saw failure at every turn. I did not know how to use my voice and felt emotionally numb. The lens of artistry that I once used to view my life was shattered and I no longer looked forward to anything. My approach to life became very passive and I kept colliding paths with the wrong people. Little did I know that my humdrum outward characterization of myself was evoking a law of attraction for unsuitable matches. I felt like a target for vagabonds, many of them searching for a gateway to attempt to control me.

I mentioned leaving judgement at the door a couple paragraphs ago when establishing that line of trust with your children. The Bible is very clear about judging others. Matthew 7 tells us, "Do not judge, or you too will be judged." This lesson was always very clear to me and I have always tried to be very kind, and not judge others who might be stamped as outcasts by critical onlookers or who are deeply misunderstood. Ironically, it has always been easy for me to judge myself while believing the insipid suitor, a Saint. I believe my "picker" was broken after becoming a victim of incest, and I did not have the first clue about how to confidently choose a partner in life but more on that later.

Being visibly passive and openly tolerant proved to be a dangerous combination and got me into trouble more than once but that was not when I became a person who settled. It was on Tuesday, September 11, 2001, when the planes hit the Twin Towers in New York and my view in Arlington was of our Pentagon engulfed in flames and smoke that I became a settler. The demise of humanity, the uncertainty of the future and unresolved trauma began my practice of settling for the wrong man and a life that was not meant to be mine.

I began sipping a light white berry mocha from Caribou Coffee at 8:15 a.m., seated at my desk at Catholic University in NE Washington, D.C. It was an out of the way stop, but Caribou Coffee in Chapel Hill, NC was the first place I discovered and began loving coffee. The love of bougie coffee is real, and that particular mocha has always remained my favorite, rich espresso intertwined with white chocolate and raspberry, topped with whipped cream, and dotted with miniature chocolate chips. Definitely not the healthiest choice but in moderation, it gave me something delicious to look forward to. The plan for the day was to close the files on Summer Opera Theatre's production of Janacek's *Jenufa*. Before me sat an impressive stack of orchestra and singer contracts, programs, fundraising event notes, to-do lists, donor information, seating charts, and volunteer lists. I had only been in my assistant role at the opera company for a few months and it was everything I hoped it would be and more.

I had two of the most fabulous ladies I have ever known as my bosses and role models at Catholic University and The Summer Opera Theatre Company. Elaine and Deanne are an unparalleled mother and daughter team whose passion for opera inspires me even more than my own. Elaine was the founder of The Summer Opera Theatre Company and had developed the company with her late husband and an impressive board of directors, delighting standing room only audiences since 1979. Deanne joined the team as a director after college, quickly showing her savvy business and organizational skills. Elaine and Deanne showed strength of character during their own afflictions, trusting to their Catholic roots, and often inspired me with their refined pedigree and lasting family traditions after adversity. I admired their innate elegance and charm; it was humble and genuine. At that time in my life, I did not fully comprehend the value of having a mentor. Elaine and Deanne were certainly two of my most treasured mentors over the years and expertly displayed the highly coveted notion of having it all. They also made it look easy and organic, showing up as the best possible version of themselves no matter if they were wearing the boss hat, mom hat, wife hat, or friend hat.

I began to sort the various stacks of documents and noticed that the Catholic University music building was unusually quiet that day. Our offices were located on the lower level of the building, and it was easy to feel off the grid, intensely focused on the project at hand. Deanne's office was around the corner from mine, I heard the phone ring, and within a moment it was obvious she had just received bad news. A few minutes later Deanne shadowed my doorway, white as a ghost, tears running down her porcelain cheeks. At 8:46 a.m. the world changed as we knew it, then again at 9:03 a.m., and 9:37 a.m., and finally 10:03 a.m.. In one hour and seventeen minutes our President was in a bunker, nineteen foreign terrorists took control of four Boeing Aircrafts, which resulted in four deadly crashes and 2,996 fatalities. Catholic University was evacuated, all routes to Virginia and Maryland were in grid lock and as I began the more than four-hour drive to my apartment, that normally would have taken 45 minutes, I wondered if I would ever truly feel safe in D.C. again. The impossible had happened and in my panicked subconscious, I felt as though the deadly event had hit the kill switch on my life in that city. In that moment, with my heart pounding and my stomach tossing, I began considering leaving D.C. and settling down in a small town. A couple of weeks later, I began dating again.

I met a variety of people in the D.C. metro area but ironically, they seemed to fit into categories which I guess should have been a big red flag. But when you come to an agreement in your mind to not die alone in D.C., you miss important details clouded by the desperation of the historical event that catapulted you into action. The first category I encountered in my quest to find a man was "the bus boys." They were creepers that I met on a commuter bus in Northern Virginia. These antisocial humans sat in the back of the bus and watched, sometimes disguising their ominous gaze with a newspaper or book but no matter, it was obvious they were uncomfortable in their own skin. These mysterious men sat fascinated, asking internal questions about the women that boarded the bus each day...where do they work, which apartment building do they live in, which stop is theirs on the Metro, and are they single? After several weeks or months of watching they muster up the courage to smile or offer their seat. Then that seed becomes a daily greeting and soon they are sitting in front or behind you on the evening commute, waiting patiently for the opportunity to casually make plans, off the bus. I made the mistake of accepting a couple of dates with these "bus boys" and soon realized that this category of men should be used for a social experiment. One man was required to ride the bus after a lifetime of chronic illegal drug use that eventually altered brain chemistry, causing daily hallucinations of imaginary Alfred Hitchcock birds aggressively diving to their deaths on his car windshield. The end result for this clown, a surrender of his car keys. The drug addiction was then replaced by a new fixation, hunting. The prey, women, and the stalking strategy was audacious. Yep, I dated that guy.

Let us chat about the man looking for inspiration for his first novel who I also met on the bus. His obsessive odyssey to become the next escape fiction author fueled his courage to adapt chapters from real life encounters. He did not have a driver's license either but his desire to remain an enigma as part of his artist persona meant I would never know why. We would walk together to restaurants in the neighborhood, and he swindled me into believing he was a creative genius. At my door he kissed me desperately, with a fist full of my hair in his hand. As he released me from the daredevil kiss, he pulled my long hair hard and fast, and I shrieked and pushed him off. His response, "I just wanted to show you who was in charge." Yep, I dated that guy too. There are a couple of lessons here. The first one, you do not have to conduct your life sitting in judgement of others, but you do have to use good common sense to avoid danger. The last place you probably want to meet someone is on the bus and the location of your home should remain private for as long as it takes to determine the existence of strong mental health of the man in question. Shortly after these two rendezvous, I began driving to work.

The second category I crossed paths with; men going through a mid-life crisis. I dated two of these characters, both of whom were more than twenty years my senior. How many novels and movies have been written about this turn of events? The man turns fifty and takes a long, lugubrious look at his life. It does not matter if his wife is a Victoria Secret model, or his children ivy leaguers. This is about him. He sees clearly defined wrinkles at the corners of his eyes, his hair is now more silver than brown, and he is quickly developing an impressive beer belly. He quickly jumps to action: joins a gym, buys new clothes (and maybe a car) and starts flirting with the twenty-something cutie in his office. They are desperate to feel the freedom that comes from being a twenty-something, freedom from aches and pains, freedom from the after-work commitments of suburban life, and freedom from feeling there is nothing to look forward to. Thankfully, these *American Beauty* variety entanglements did not last long, and I was able to escape in one piece. The very obvious lesson I would like to share, do not waste your time on a category of men who is clearly looking for a quick fix to forget the impasse of growing older. These dudes have decades of experience to lure you in with fancy dinners and over-the-top floral arrangements, but you will soon find that their attraction is mostly superficial, grabbing at straws for anything that makes them feel young again.

Growing older is something I have always embraced with gratitude. I suppose because my mortality was hanging by a thread at age twenty. I believe I became an "old soul" and therefore related to people who were older because of my own life experiences. It is not always bad to date someone significantly older than you. My husband is nine years older than me, and our relationship is a fairy tale. One older man I dated after my battle with cancer taught me a lot about myself and using adversity for inspiration in artistic expression first in my music and now, in my writing.

I had just returned from cancer treatment and was beginning my senior year at Elon University. I met Doug at a bookstore that we both worked at part-time. Doug was also a college professor and cared deeply for humans from all walks of life. He was seventeen years my senior and the age difference made my family nervous, but I can say confidently there was never an ulterior motive. Coming back to my life after cancer had me trapped between childhood and independent living as an adult. Doug provided a safe place to begin dating and treated me like a lady. Doug was tall and slender, always wore jeans, black chucks and carried himself with an aura of mystery. First impressions told me he was gentle, unconventionally charming, and unconditionally kind. Doug was modest, never taking credit for the effortless laughs his scintillating humor produced. He was always available for a friend or student. He was also a very attentive and devoted Dad to his son, Jordan. He was so proud to be a father and watching the two of them together gave me so much joy.

Doug loved music and it was part of him, maybe even more so than music was a part of me. Many of our dates were spent sitting outside listening to Emmy Lou Harris, Miles Davis, and Mary Margaret O'Hara on a Sony discman while watching traffic in the distance on Interstate 40. Doug would close his eyes and allow the music to wash over him, the meaning and melodies would fill the chambers of longing in his soul. Music was his medicine and seemed to heal the pain of loss. The action of accepting the music, which is a very apathetic activity for many of us, was truly an out of body experience for him. It made me almost envious to watch him connect so completely to art in multiple genres. He was giddy as a child whenever he discovered a new artist, a soulful musician with something relevant to say. He paid attention to all of it and was more "in the moment" of his life than anyone I had ever known.

Doug was also an accomplished poet. I was honored when he asked to write a poem about me that was eventually published in *Washington Square* magazine in the summer of 2003. The poem fascinated me, and admittedly also baffled me. It begins with the experience of taking in an oratorio aria and more than that, the vocal mechanics of what it takes to deliver said aria. The poem also mentions the biopsy scars on my body and a brief mention of the hallucination I experienced during chemotherapy. Doug saw the world and the many pieces of an otherwise typical experience almost like a radiologist examining an x-ray. There were elements present that the untrained eye would miss but he got it all, every profound detail and created art that was a gift to the world. He saw me, perhaps better than I saw myself and appreciated the art I expressed, realizing what a gift it was to be able to continue to sing after cancer that resided in my neck. Our relationship was largely platonic, and not sexual in nature which was just what I needed in that time of my life. I always felt loved and safe.

One afternoon we were filing books at work and I asked Doug why he loved me. His answer, "I am drawn to you because you are broken." His response knocked the wind out of me. My mind raced with what that could possibly mean. *Did he view me as emotionally fractured by my recent experience with cancer? Was he referring to my scar covered neck and chest?* I could not ask him what he meant as my fear got the best of me, but years of self-reflection have allowed me to draw my own conclusions. I mentioned earlier that I thought my "picker" was broken after I left New Orleans. Maybe that was no accident, perhaps the existence of brokenness is actually a protective measure to allow us the time to do the work of recovery after trauma. Looking back to that conversation with Doug, I want to believe that he was speaking to how being broken by an experience somehow gives us the strength to be better than we ever would have been if we had been spared. I believe he had strong opinions about perspective and that being broken by adversity gives us a voice to affect the lives of others.

I have learned over the years that serious writers are often praying for life experience that will provide inspiration to put pen to paper. I believe Doug was guiding me with tough love to do something profound with my experience, to leave an original imprint on the world. I have had a lot of traumas and am no longer going to live as a fragile bird, settling for a cryptic life hidden in the shadows of shameful secrets. I am going to take flight and use these life experiences as an opportunity to help others and free myself from the burden of my past bad luck. I will no longer waste time attempting to crack the code on my cipher of misfortune. I am going to use my voice and my pen to give hope to strangers and most importantly, guidance to the seven amazing children I am lucky enough to call mine. That is how we take our power back after we are broken by an experience. We use our voice and stand up proud as survivors with battle scars that remind us every single day that we are stronger than the demon who tried to take us down. What if we instead became centered on the lessons that come from the hardship? Character building is developed in many ways and sometimes the most influential and impactful growth comes from periods of oppression.

I think Doug saw the potential in me to have a deeply poignant life. The potential to change the future for other people through my own life lessons. I met Doug at age twenty-one and was not mature enough to interpret his balladry. Professors often try to guide students to their own discoveries; however, I was still too close to the fire of adversity to see how it could be used for good. I wish I could call him and thank him for inspiring me to write it all down. It was Doug who planted the original seed that is now blossoming into a beautiful future, free from the traumas that controlled me for decades. I learned recently that Doug died a couple of years ago. I am certain he had so much more he wanted to say but for now I am including his beautiful poem and picture as a treasured memorial to a man who touched the lives of so many and, most importantly, to a beloved son who called his father, "hero."

Doug Smith, 1998

"Once I loved an opera singer with great
passion, this poem rises from the mystery of
her voice. Language allows us to be human.
The world threatens to overwhelm us, so we
tell a story about the overwhelming world.
There is darkness, so we tell a story about
the desire for light." ~ Douglas Smith

Fugitive Notes on Certain Cantatas
for Allison, singing
Douglas Smith
Let her mouth flower, at night, into forms of praise
Let the measured voice, the petals of tongue and breath,
scale the sky to render a stigmata of stars.
Let the throat's weather deliver benedictions
in rising rain. The world drowning, describes an ark
of breath, an aria in bone. To shape our fear
she fashions prayer in membranes of sound. To a maze
of distance she sings. Silence is buried, like death,
in each ecstatic note. There is nothing like scars
to mark the body. Listen deeper: the fictions
of music and order, the sea voice swimming dark,
tell us to drown, with variations, in the ear

*   *   *   *

I have always been a glass is half full kind of gal. Of course
the glass broke several times over the years, but I was always
able to start fresh with a new glass once I processed, actually
suppressed, the situation. I guess you could say this book is
my testament to remaining positive no matter how many
new glasses you have to fill. My first husband has always
been a glass is half empty person and it always affected our
marriage. I mentioned that I settled for him after my incestuous trauma and my world is going to end mentality
following 911. We did have things in common, but our core
values were not aligned and that should have been a deal
breaker. The truth is, he falls into the target audience for
this book as he has been smacked hard by adversity. He lost
his parents in his teens and early twenties, his first wife left
him, then I left him, and he has had his own serious medical
problems over the years. I stayed with him for seven years
and in that time, we had two perfect children. I will always
be indebted to him for making me a mother but hope one
day he will find happiness and freedom from his own hard-
ships. The lesson here, if your partner is permanently stuck

in the past, unwilling to address the issues that are holding him captive, and his daily existence is painted with cynicism there is no way to move forward together in my humble opinion. I am happy to share that we have a very healthy co-parenting relationship and our two children are thriving!

The final category of clowns I ran across in D.C., the quiet, unassuming friend of a friend but I will need all of Chapter 5 to tell you about that.

LIFE LESSON #4
Embrace solitude and do not settle.

Listen up friend, you are a beautiful, smart, courageous person who has so much to offer another person, the right person. Do your research, figure out what you truly want and wait for him or her. Do not settle after the next terrorist attack because you believe the world is about to end. Do not settle because your younger sister got married last year and your family is whispering about you at family events. Do not settle because your biological clock is ticking at age twenty-seven and you do not think they will ever show up. I have several friends who became mothers after the age of forty, so stop worrying. God always has a plan. I did not meet my soul mate until I was thirty-four years old but, sister, it was like God was flashing an enormous, green, blinking arrow directly over him when we met. Wait for the man who is truly smitten with you, the man who makes you feel like the only woman in the room, or in the universe for that matter. The man who tells you he thinks you are gorgeous, even with no make-up. The man who cannot wait to grab you up into his arms and kiss you after a long day. And finally, the man who tells you he loves and cherishes you every single day. You will know, I promise.

Right now, focus on you. Who are you? What do you want to learn and focus on in your own personal growth? What are your goals? Take a cooking class. Buy a bike and ride the trails every Sunday. Start a list of books you have been wanting to read and commit to one per month. Join a growth group at your church. Plan a trip to an exciting destination with your best friend. This is your time, and your perfect match will show up when you least expect it. If you have been trapped, settling for a dismal life because of unresolved trauma it is time to take action! You do not have to suffer as a victim of your circumstances, you can take your power back at any time.

Sigmund Freud once said, "I think this man is suffering from memories," when discussing trauma. As someone who allowed the trauma reel to loop while clamped down in suppression for decades, I know this sort of suffering all too well. The suffering sometimes felt like being broken.

The idea of being broken is very off putting for most of us but what if it was actually an opportunity? What if the break in our foundation provided space for you to finally discover truth and move past the lies, providing safe transport to your destiny? You are currently occupying that space with anxiety, depression, and a negative inner dialogue you cannot turn off. Be brave and take charge of the situation so you are not vulnerable to accept the affection of someone who is not worthy of you. The transformation that casts us from trauma, outfitted with iron clad truth, allows us to live a legacy of hope after adversity.

* * * *

The transformation that casts us from trauma, outfitted with iron clad truth, allows us to live a legacy of hope after adversity.

* * * *

So, what have we learned? There are a lot of schmucks out there and sadly, we typically date a lot of them until we meet "the one." I know dating can be draining but if you do not do the research, you cannot make an informed decision. I mentioned in the first paragraph that I was intrigued by why clowns would choose a profession (or hobby) that allows them to remain anonymous. I am sure there are a variety of answers to that question which is fine. But if you are dating someone who is navigating your relationship incognito, that should set off alarms. If they are unwilling to reveal themselves to you and parts of their life are cloaked in mystery, I would advise you to do a full investigation before allowing yourself to fall for them. My suggestion is take your time and figure out what you want.

Make your list of what you are looking for in your soul mate and beyond the physical. What does his character look like? Is he generous? Does he volunteer and help his community? Is he kind, like help the elderly to their car and unload their groceries, kind? Is he a leader, does he inspire those around him? Is he driven and a goal setter? Is he passionate about hobbies that define and fulfill him? What attributes do not matter? Who cares if he is not tall or has blond hair instead of brown? Dig deep sister! And, when you do date a jackass, do not cry for weeks over him when it ends. Give yourself one night. Listen to "your song" and then delete it from your play list. Cry it out while watching your favorite "Rom Com" and devouring the entire pint of Cherry Garcia. Then brush your teeth, wash your face, and go to sleep. Wake up the next day and start a new journey as a wiser, more fabulous you! Jump out of the bed, hit the Starbucks, buy a new outfit at TJ Maxx, and plan a fun night out with your friends. But do not, I repeat do not, spend one more moment crying over that unsuitable clown! It is not always fun to be alone, but that solitude will teach you so much, I promise you that!

It took me a few years, but I realize now that I thought solitude and loneliness were the same thing, they are not. Belgian-American Poet May Sarton tells us, "Loneliness is the poverty of self; solitude is the richness of self." Wow, so solitude can be a good thing and we have a choice of how we view and utilize the time we are alone. This was a big "aha! moment" for me and suddenly I felt triggered into action. My time alone was a gift and I needed to treat it as such. I had a boyfriend once who moved across the country. Jason decided to get to know his new city at his own pace and read a tall stack of books in his solitude. He knew no one in his new city but allowed the quiet parts of his week to be filled with his love of learning and the more social parts to develop organically. Wait, what?

What if we used our time of solitude and reflection to learn something new, explore new passions or become more mindful through prayer or meditation? Instead of binge watching *The Office* for the hundredth time, we should get off the couch, take a walk, buy a new book, and shine the light on a more dynamic person. What did you do when your last relationship broke up? Did you immediately create a fabulous profile on match.com or eharmony.com? We all crave that surge of confidence that comes from a wink or message from a potential match but let us be real, are you really going to be ready to jump into a new relationship while mourning the one you just lost? Take some time for yourself, my sister, and see what that gift of time will mean for your future. You are an amazing creation and God has exciting plans for you!

CHAPTER 5
M E T O O

What does childhood nostalgia feel like to you? Better yet, what does it feel, smell, look, and taste like? Last week I drove by my Grandma and Granddaddy's house in Roanoke, Virginia. The humble brick Cape Cod looked like it had a fresh coat of paint, but it was the same and suddenly I was flooded with memories of my pre-teens and my visits there. My grandparents have been dead for over twenty years, but I still find a reason to drive by that house a couple times each year. Being with Grandma and Granddaddy, my Mom's parents, was always a wonderfully predictable experience and I loved that. I can remember Kiki and I running around their backyard between tomato bushes and laundry lines taking in the sweet honeysuckle fragrance as we attempted to catch our breath. On rainy days we would rock on the big green front porch swing watching the boxwood bushes for spiders or play in the rustic basement that still had a dirt floor and housed many treasures from World War II. Dinner was always served around the dining room table at six p.m. followed by an hour of silence as we would not dare interrupt *Wheel of Fortune* or *Jeopardy*.

We slept in the twin room, and I remember the two beds were tall and slightly rickety. Sleep was always effortless in their home. The nightly routine included closing my eyes to the distant chirp of crickets, quiet flickering of lightening bugs and a cool breeze from the open window that made the white linen curtains dance. The next morning my Grandma would wake us with the delicious aroma of baked honey buns accompanied by a tall glass of milk. My grandparents lived in the middle of the city, but it still felt like the safest place on earth. As I look back on those simple days, I realize how much I took for granted, the pre-teen years were easy, peaceful, and quiet. How many times during the deadly storms that mangled parts of my life have I prayed for quiet and peaceful? Too many to count. Always remember to appreciate and see the value of wishful and lonely frames of time as you may look back and realize that the thing you were craving could be the very thing that ends up destroying you.

* * * *

Always remember to appreciate and see the value of wishful and lonely frames of time as you may look back and realize that the thing you were craving could be the very thing that ends up destroying you.

* * * *

I met him through friends I sang with at my church job of all places. I was living a very happy existence in Northern Virginia and worked at a small opera company in North East D.C. I was also singing every weekend for two agencies for weddings, funerals, corporate engagements, and oratorio gigs. I had just received a promotion at my primary job. The new role at the opera company was administrative director, and I helped launch and maintain a young professionals group called "The Mozart Circle." The goal was to engage individuals in their twenties and thirties to learn about and hopefully learn to love opera the way I did. The next Mozart Circle event was scheduled just before Valentine's Day, and I was going to lead a discussion on the great love stories in opera over cocktails and appetizers.

I met the general manager in the primitive event room on the 3rd floor of a three-story restaurant venue and immediately my mind began to brainstorm ideas for props and décor to spice up the venue. It was without a doubt a very laid-back atmosphere that I hoped would make the attendees more comfortable as I attempted to engage them with stories I loved. Although, for anyone outside of the opera world, the tales would read a bit dated. I imagine, therefore, this to be the cause of why opera is a dying art. The stories must continue to be told though beautiful music and exquisite sets over decades but sadly, the stories become lost on younger generations and the sets, too expensive to reproduce year after year with dwindling attendance and ghosted financial resources. My passion for bridging the gap was rich with purpose and I could not wait to tell my bosses and board of directors about the exciting upcoming event. I descended the two flights of stairs to the hole in the wall bar on the ground floor, even more rustic than the event room, and almost forgot I had agreed to a date following the meeting. My date was sitting at the bar sipping a Stella in a slightly spotted glass. His name was Ethan.

Ethan sat on a rustic wooden stool with his back toward me. He was dressed in jeans and a plaid button-down shirt; he carried a vintage satchel as he had come straight from work. Ethan was attractive in a nerdy sort of way, but his pretentiousness was visible before I even saw his face. The truth is I was honestly underwhelmed by him as it was quickly apparent, he held himself in a high regard and his obvious arrogance was a big turn off to me. Ethan was highly educated but used it to make others feel small; it did not take me long to figure this out. He would flex his brain muscle in conversations to make himself seem more interesting. It made him seem more boring, and insecure truth be told.

Furthermore, kindness has always been more important to me than a dazzling intellect. Anyone can read a book and talk about it at a party but an individual who takes the time to listen and connect with another human in a meaningful way has always made me weak in the knees.

Ethan always wanted to be around me, even when I was at gigs. This should have been a big red flag but after dating a bunch of players over the years who toyed with my emotions with games, I was excited someone wanted to spend time with me. One night I was hired to sing a wedding at a big fancy hotel in Baltimore and I had recruited Bryce, my friend I met at opera camp several summers before, to sing a duet with me. Bryce had a gorgeous tenor voice; an exhilarating laugh and sincere warmth that was often lacking in the opera world. I was excited to sing "The Prayer" with him, the song made famous by Celine Dion and Andrea Bocelli. It was a black-tie wedding; Bryce wore a black tuxedo and patent leather dress shoes. I wore a black satin evening gown with black strappy heels, my hair was pinned on the right side with a pearl and rhinestone hair pin that matched my earrings.

By the time of the Baltimore gig, I guess you could say I was in a relationship with Ethan. I had allowed the shiny wrapping paper that curtained his know-it-all personality be the reason to keep him in my life. He insisted upon driving me the eighty minutes to Baltimore as he feared for my safety or at least that is the story he told me. The hotel was in the heart of the downtown area, and it was not the safest neighborhood but was the definition of elegance as soon as you entered the glitzy revolving door. I thought it was very chivalrous that he wanted to drive me but boy was I wrong. Bryce and I began our rehearsal and Ethan watched from the back of the ballroom, standing beside a picture window draped in gold velvet floor length curtains. The expansive crystal chandelier shifted slightly during the sound check and I remember thinking it was the most stunning room I had ever seen. Twenty black clothed circular tables accompanied by eight gold latter backed chairs made the expansive room feel intimate during a pre-pandemic time where a wedding of less than two hundred was unheard of in the D.C. metro area.

The pianist began the intro and I felt myself come alive, spurred on by the excitement of performing in the gorgeous, resounding space. The harmony of mine and Bryce's voices filled the impressive room, and my skin swelled with goosebumps. I remember hoping our performance would put the cherry on top of a perfect wedding day for the bride and groom. I had not yet met the prematrimonial couple, as they had hired me through an agency sight unseen. Ethan interrupted us with a needy call of my name asking me to cut the rehearsal short. I do not know if Ethan was threatened by our chemistry (it is called acting) or the fact that he had no control over the situation, but he decided to have a full-on hissy fit in the middle of the ballroom. He demanded to be invited to attend the wedding and watch our performance live. I explained I was hired for the gig and the contract did not say, "Feel free to bring your obnoxious boyfriend." He proceeded to find the bar and got stumbling, slurring, sloppy drunk. Bryce cautioned me and said I needed to take a long hard look at the relationship. I wish I had listened.

I love dessert. Okay, not *every* dessert but the ones I do love, the love is real! I am not a fan of the traditional birthday cake with the buttercream icing, for example. In my travels over the years, I have been able to identify my favorites. On Valentine's Day last year my sweet husband took me to "Brentwood" in Little River (a suburb of Myrtle Beach) and we enjoyed baked oysters and crab stuffed lobster, but the main event was the chocolate soufflé complete with a deliciously tart raspberry coulis. This prodigious dessert rivalled the soufflés we enjoyed in Paris two years before. The unique texture and delicate sweetness felt regal, and the experience an exclusive one. Best of all the restaurant is haunted and the Maître D' loves to share stories of the sightings and recalled a recent ghostly event where the bus boy was greeted inside the walk-in cooler by a ghost and was never quite the same. I am fascinated by the history of places like "Brentwood" and how apparitions get grounded in a space in our world trapped between times and dimensions. Perhaps I will be a ghost hunter in my next life, who knows?

My absolute favorite dessert to date can be found at "44 West" located at the Greenbrier Resort in West Virginia. The Wagyu steak and lobster mashed potatoes, which were featured on *The Best Thing I Ever Ate* are also not to be missed. My favorite dessert ever, hands down, is the 44 West bananas foster and the experience is unforgettable. The charming southern-twanged server rolls a gorgeous gold and mahogany cart to your table where she artfully assembles and flambés the bananas, brown sugar, cinnamon, and vanilla in dark rum. The dessert artist then pours the wonderfully fragrant blend of sugary deliciousness over vanilla bean ice cream and a homemade coconut pound cake. I have dreams about this dessert and have learned to only order a four-ounce steak in order to save room. It is worth every bit of the calories; I promise you that!

The following weekend I invited Ethan to attend a chorale performance I was singing in at my church. Our mutual friends were all going to be there, and the plan was to go out to the local Irish pub after the event. The performance was a great success, and we had a full house in the audience. My singing buddies and I were excited to go out to celebrate after singing our hearts out. It was late so we were planning to do appetizers and drinks. I decided to order the Baileys cheesecake as I had a late lunch. I was absolutely stunned when Ethan whispered in my ear, "Do you really need to eat that, Ally?" It was not the first time he had referred to my weight in a negative way. Granted I was not a size two but I was healthy and comfortable at 5'6" at a size eight. I had never had anyone criticize my weight or try to tell me what to order in a restaurant before, but I knew I did not like it. I went home that night and started making my list of pros and cons as Bryce had suggested. Oh, and in case you are wondering, I most certainly enjoyed every single bite of that piece of cheesecake.

The next week I came down with a cold. I had a low-grade fever, sinus congestion and a nagging cough. I decided to stay in my apartment that weekend to get well. I loved that little apartment. It was on the top floor of a small one-building complex and you could see Washington National Cathedral above the trees in the distance. One entire wall was made up of windows and made the studio apartment space feel voluminous. There was an accordion door separating the bedroom and main living space and the tiny kitchen and bathroom had just been remodeled before I moved in. Across the street was an enchanting French café and around the corner, a Lebanese taverna. I loved living in an "International" neighborhood, experiencing the cultures and cuisines of faraway countries. Working for a non-profit and being a struggling performer did not allow for many extras or a large living space, but I sure did love my little piece of heaven and the many interesting people I met in that diverse community.

Just as I was about to get ready for bed, Ethan surprised me at my door with hot chicken noodle soup. It was very thoughtful, but I just wanted to be alone and go to sleep. I thanked him for bringing it and said I would eat it the next day as I was about to go to sleep. He asked if he could hang out while I slept and for some reason, I said, "Okay." He plopped himself in front of the TV and I went to bed. At two a.m. I awoke to unequivocal confusion and terror. I was laying on my stomach, confused and groggy from cold medicine. At first, I thought I was having a dream as I had been sound asleep. I felt him behind me, assuming he was kissing me goodnight I raised my head to meet his lips. I quickly became aware that he was under the covers, naked. My night gown shifted during sleep and was around my waist, revealing my own nakedness. Then suddenly, without a word, I felt a sharp surge of pain, all of him, every inch was inside of me. Ethan raped me and not in the way you would imagine. That barbarian raped me through "the back door," and it was awful. I felt as though all remaining innocence was violently snatched, like he had nothing in the world to lose. It did not last long but long enough to inflict pain like I had never experienced before. He used a few savage thrusts to prove to me, and to himself, that he was in control. He collapsed beside me and passed out when he was finished with me.

I laid there, emotionally numb, unable to process being a victim of another sexual violation. This was the answer to every question I was asking myself about him. He did not want to love me, he wanted to bridle me like a wild horse. He wanted power, that was it. Ethan had attempted to dominate me with his verbal commands without my compliance. He adjusted his manipulation strategy into physical action and because he lacked any recognizable humanity or compassion, it was easy for him. Ethan was undoubtedly a sociopath, unable to display basic human emotion and had no understanding or regard for empathy. There was a big black hole where his heart should have resided. Vice President, Kamala Harris said it best, "Predators are cowards." Ethan was the worst kind of coward as he could not even look me in the face and waited to rape me until I was unarmed on cold medicine. Ethan knew that I would feel humiliated which would be enough to gag me and keep the secret that he is the worst kind of demon safe. Today, however; I get the last laugh because my story is out and I am not ashamed, I am proud of my courage to share it.

Minutes after the attack, I felt blood running down my inner thigh and quietly made my way to the bathroom. I was wearing a delicate white traditional nightgown that fell to my mid-calf that my Aunt Phyllis and Uncle Darryl had given me the Christmas before. The gown was modest and had lovely ribbon detail at the square neck. My Aunt Phyllis and Uncle Darryl always found the most thoughtful gifts and the gown was one of my favorites. I turned in the mirror to find the nightgown completely defaced, stained with my own blood and I sunk to the ground and had a panic attack. This was my first bona fide panic attack; I do not count the drunken stooper in New Orleans as it was charged with the overindulgence of Jack Daniels. My heart was beating so loud and fast that I thought I was having a heart attack. I could not catch my breath and tears were flowing at an alarming rate down my face. My mind was flooded with questions and the hateful inner dialogue that haunted me from New Orleans was as loud as ever. Why did I wait so long to end it? How did I miss that he was the Devil? Why did I not make the list before it was too late? Why did I ignore all the signs? What do I do now? How will I ever wrap my mind around being defiled this way?

I cleaned myself up, changed into my bath robe and buried my beautiful nightgown deep in the trash can. I spent the whole night on the cold floor of my bathroom, waiting to confront him as soon as the sun came up. A hundred eyes were on me as I looked up at the rubber ducky shower curtain. I felt judged, not by the duckies but by my subconscious, asking why I never processed the sexual abuse in New Orleans. The absence of a therapeutic process in New Orleans meant I could not fully identify this evil doer until it was too late. This was a vicious attack and was so much worse than anything that had ever happened to me. I had been savagely sodomized and was covered in my own blood. I felt like I was part of a satanic crime scene, attacked by the Devil himself, and that day would forever be marked in my memory as the worst day of my life.

The next morning was rough. I was emotionally tormented by Ethan's violent plunder that was replaying in my mind like a horror film, and in unimaginable pain both mentally and physically. I was desperate to believe it had all been a bad dream. Ethan came into the bathroom looking for me around seven a.m. The nightmare became worse when he told me it was an accident, and he did not realize what he had done. He was like a selfish deserter in a war, a ridiculous chicken who had to play dumb with a deer in the headlights expression because he was not man enough to admit it. I kicked him out and told him to stay away from me or I would press charges. He knew what he was doing, this was all planned, he was exerting his power over me after weeks of what he viewed as my disobedience. I was about to embark on a journey with my five stages of grief with a long layover in angry town. I was furious. I wanted to beat the living hell out of him but knew in my rational mind (what little of it was present) that I needed to stay away from him. A couple weeks later I am told he moved several hours South for a fresh start. Interesting, why would you abruptly move if you had no guilt, no fault, or no intention? He was gone, and I was left to pick up the pieces of my battered body and fractured soul without acceptable closure.

The sad reality, I did not pick up the pieces. I did my due diligence and went to a doctor to make sure I was physically okay. She was very understanding and compassionate but instead of therapy she prescribed a dangerous band-aide called Xanax. I took it for longer than I should have. Xanax is a benzodiazepine and is highly addictive. It works with the brain and central nervous system to produce a calming effect and thankfully I never got addicted. The effect of Xanax, however; did cause me to make decisions I never would have made had I chosen therapy instead. I was on Xanax when I met my first husband. I was blind to all the red flags. When he told me I was not his type, subtly criticizing my physical appearance. When he dropped me off at the emergency room with a severe kidney infection and went to a party without me. When he flirted with other women and deserted me at events we attended together, ignoring me completely. I was not number one, I probably was not even number 5 in his eyes. He was always looking for something or someone better. But my pal Xanax convinced me he was "the one" because I thought the euphoria I felt was bearing fruit from our love. The euphoria was budding from an extremely affective buzz from my Xanax fix. I took Xanax off and on for several months but if I could do it again, I would 100% always choose therapy instead.

Looking back on it now, I am so grateful to God for giving me the courage to speak up about my sexual abuse. I think about the newly identified predators that have been outed this year, the Jeffrey Epstein's, and Keith Raniere's of the world who are finally facing justice. How does ferocious predatory behavior begin? Did these nefarious individuals ever have empathy, or did the exploitation of innocent women come easy? How in this world did the recent infamous beasts of prey get away with the sexual abuse of underage minors? Or years of cultish mind manipulation that lead to the disfigurement of strong, smart women whose only crime was trusting the wrong man. I feel a deep connection to the brave souls, their victims, who have been able to find freedom, using their own heroic voices. I am indebted to all the courageous women who stood up proudly this year and every year since 2017 and said, "Me too." Sometimes it takes years, or in my case two decades, to share the horror of being raped but I truly hope it inspires other women to speak bravely about their own assaults and to find freedom in truth and justice.

I mentioned earlier that tigers are very solitary creatures. I relate to this as I feel being brutally raped and sexually abused catapulted me into a state of seclusion. Not to mention the battle with cancer and the death of my first love. I believed it was difficult for others to understand surviving that magnitude of hardship in just a couple of years so I isolated myself and held it all inside. I had a falling out with my primary friend group many years ago. During the dismantle I remember accusing one of the girls of never being supportive of me and my past traumas. Her response, "I am being as supportive as you will allow me to be." She was exactly right. I had shut down and was completely closed off to anyone who would try to help me. Solitude is powerful and necessary for sorting out our feelings and healing, but we cannot permanently live there. I fear that I have lived there for two decades because it felt safe.

During this specific time of solitude, I felt hopelessly alone and found myself hating men. I desperately wished I could rewrite my story as I did not recognize myself anymore. I had become a recluse. I had also become dangerously sad and confined to my apartment. I needed help. All the anguish had me spiraling with anxiety fraught with regular panic attacks. I also considered hurting myself although I had no plan to carry it out. I was falling into a dark depression and had not the first idea of how to climb out of my pit of despair. Finally, after no motivation and sleeping my way through a couple of weeks, I reemerged and adopted a couple of cats. I did not want to be around people, but cats seemed harmless enough and just the comfort and company I so desperately needed at that moment in time. I named my feline saviors Gabriel and Raphael and their angelic love was most certainly heaven sent. Between the animal therapy and the on and off use of Xanax I began to feel better and decided to hire a therapist.

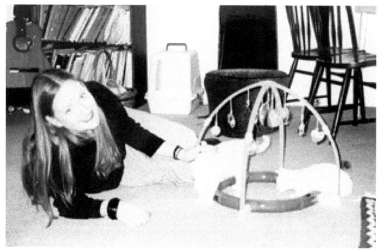

Ally with "the angels", 2003

I have seen therapists on and off since I was nineteen years old. I believe in therapy, but you must do the work. Therapists have an arsenal of tools designed to help you work through trauma. The more you engage and participate, the better you feel. I also believe in medication, the appropriate medication, and it is not a weakness to admit you need it. I tried to fix my anxiety and past traumas with lifestyle changes, but it never stuck. I once asked someone what their first impression was of me. I was stunned to hear that they always viewed me as "keyed up and charged with anxiety." That was not the impression, first or otherwise, that I wanted to put out into the world. I thought I was hiding it all so well behind my forced smile, but the truth is, that smile lacked authenticity. And behind closed doors I was an absolute mess. I began experiencing the symptoms of my "traumaniacal" self after the incest, but the reoccurrence of the manifestation continued for two decades. Two decades, 20+ years of racing heartbeats, night sweats, uncontrollable shaking, waterfall thoughts of loss and fear, drinking to excess to numb my feelings, over-eating all the remaining feelings, and hating myself.

Five years ago, my doctor suggested an anti-depressant after observing the physical signs of my out-of-control anxiety. I tried Zoloft and it worked for me. It took the edge off the feeling that a panic attack was right around the corner. It allowed me to finally sleep through the night. It allowed me to think logically and not worry that something would happen to one of my children every time they left the house. It gave me more control over my emotions and from taking my distress out on my nails or cuticles. It gave me better focus to put my attention on God, my husband, and my children. It allowed the fog of anxiety and depression to subside so I could do the work on all the trauma that was resurfacing year after year.

Anxiety and depression continue to have a stigma attached to them. I saw an interview with a famous model recently and she seemed embarrassed to share her struggle with crippling anxiety. Why are we so afraid to talk about this? Good God, there are a thousand things to be worried about in our current world so there is no surprise in my mind that forty million adults in the United States suffer with anxiety. I say suffer because 63% of those struggling with anxiety are not receiving treatment of any kind…no medicine, no therapy, nothing! I have talked a lot about signs, and I feel like God gave me a sign when I hit rock bottom (a second time) and almost hurt myself. The good news, my friend, is that you do not have to wait to hit rock bottom, you can make the decision to address your anxiety right now! Dig into your Bible and talk to God. Get online and find a therapist at psychologytoday.com or call your primary care physician and discuss options. I know it can seem scary but the freedom from the heavy chains of anxiety and depression outweighs the fear, I promise you that!

Jesus reminds us we have hope in God in Matthew 11:28-30. God wants us to reach out to him in crisis, all we must do is talk to him.

Matthew 11:28-30
"Come to me, all you who are weary and burdened, and I will give you rest. Take my yoke upon you, and learn from me, because I am gentle and humble in heart, and you will find rest for your souls. For my yoke is easy, and my burden is light."

LIFE LESSON #5
Always eat dessert and trust your intuition.

I am a rape victim, and that is unforgivable. I do not blame myself, but there were signs that he was not a good match for me (or anyone else in their right mind.) Please learn from my example and if something seems off, it probably is. Trust your intuition! Everyone has faults but if your man is trying to change who you are, that is a deal breaker. God loves who you are, and he created you to be you, not who your toxic boyfriend thinks you should be. Also, life is short so eat the darn dessert. Maybe not every day, but once a week (or month) celebrate with the cake you love, or whatever your thing is. Life is supposed to be enjoyed so appreciate the little things even if in moderation.

For five months the paragraph above was the end of this chapter. I knew there was much more to say but the idea of discussing all the raw lacerations that Ethan left behind felt insurmountable. Yet here we are, and I am about to share way beyond my comfort zone. My goal with what I am about to tell you, is to model how to #stayfierce and what the valiant veracity of exposing our most tender wounds feels like. It feels like freedom and eventually gives way to healing but the ground plan to get there is complicated. You can see democracy in the distance, the aroma of your newfound independence is delicious, like nectarous restitution or spicy due process. We have all played judge and jury with cases and causes that coil us up in a tizzy when justice is not served. Sometimes the constitutionality of the crime committed does not always make sense to the uninformed observer and that is why, in part, the continuation of this chapter is difficult for me.

You would think that being brutally sodomized while sleeping is one of the worst things one person can do to another person outside of attempted murder. In most cases I would agree but Ethan took much more than my remaining innocence from me. I need to take you back to when I first started my graduate program at Loyola. I was studying music performance with a concentration in opera, but the foundation of that degree was firmly rooted with music theory and music history. In music history we did a lot of writing and I loved telling the stories of composers and their influences through picturesque imagery. I always got A's on my writing while at Elon and Loyola but I did not aspire to become Anne Rice's protégé by any means. Honestly, I had no idea how writing would become important but that is where the seed was planted. For several years I would tinker with writing, on the small scale with journaling and when I was feeling adventurous, I would write a detailed story about a milestone event in my life. Being a writer never seemed like something I was meant to do until my therapeutic process led me here, and now I have never felt more certain.

Being in a relationship with a sociopath is like taking a one-way trip to the ocean's Twilight Zone. You are trapped below the surface, but the sunlight is just beyond your reach. This layer of water is murky and is characterized by a high existence of jellyfish. Sociopaths are resourceful and they have mastered the art of clouding your vision to only see what they want you to see and their sting is so subtle, it may go unnoticed at first. They are antisocial and controlling. They do not understand right or wrong nor do they wish to understand either or both. They do not care about the feelings of others. They have no guilt and lying comes easy. The action of manipulating others is a daily endeavor and most of the time they are experts at it. I already shared that Ethan attempted to diminish my confidence by implying that I was overweight. That slippery suggestion was obvious and was returned with a figurative middle finger when I devoured the entire slice of cheesecake while he watched with an evil eye pout. He was smarter than I gave him credit for because his second manipulation took hold and left scars.

Ethan studied me, always looking for a crack, a way to get in and manage me. He looked for weakness and one day he found the source of mine. I think he observed the anxiety in me before I fully saw it in myself. He also knew what button to push to set my budding anxiety into motion, down a very steep cliff. It started with the surface observations and criticism and with in weeks he was insulting my intellect. I am not sure how he convinced me that I was stupid, but I remember clearly that my fear of others thinking it ramped up my anxiety to daily visits without warning. I recall having a conversation with a board member at the opera company and would second guess every word that came out of my mouth, obsessing about overusing the same adjectives. I would be hosting an event and get tongue tied during the welcome greeting, unable to manage a coherent thought. It was as if I had been cursed and it was easy to believe the lies because the follow up to the mental attack was the sodomized rape.

Ethan had managed to convince me that I was fat and dumb (I imagine those are the descriptors he would use) and then he raped me in the most atrocious way imaginable. I have felt unworthy of many things in my life as it pertains to my intellectual dexterity but that ends today. I mentioned earlier that justice looks different to everyone, especially those of us who have a horse in the race. I am sure my fierce fellow rape survivors who may or may not have experienced some part or all of this are wondering why I did not prosecute him. There are many days where I ask myself the same question. In a few chapters you will read my thoughts on passion and purpose but the procurement of justice in this chapter works hand in hand with what I believe to be God's purpose for my life.

The night after I was raped, I stayed up all night, armed with a kitchen knife that I thought about using on myself. The tears were constant, my chest was strained from relentless anxiety, and my voice was hoarse from sobbing. The triggered anxiety kept flashing the same ideas to my overstimulated consciousness. The merciless wheel spun round and round until I was dizzy, but the message read clear as day...I was a fat, ugly, stupid, defiled tramp who got what was coming to her. This atrocious narrative had been developing ever since I was abused by Stan and I allowed myself to believe it. You are probably wondering how justice and purpose fit into all of this? Well...as I told you earlier, Ethan was counting on my shame to keep me quiet so in his sick, demented mind he believed he got away with his cowardly attack. Justice is divided into two pieces in this story. First, I am taking my power back by telling my story and saving other women from potential attacks and/or abuse. And second, I am sure God is going to direct me to a publishing home for this story where I can prove that I am an intelligent woman with valuable things to say and that no insidious sociopath will ever attempt to break or muzzle me again. Thank you for reading this story, I am blessed by the ability to be able to protect others by sharing my wisdom. Stay fierce my friend, and trust that intuition!

Update: God is good and justice is beautiful… I have been presented with three traditional publishing offers, my voice is finally free and I am proud!

CHAPTER 6
THE
MIGHTY
RIVER

I ran across a John Wayne quote recently: "Courage is being scared to death…and saddling up anyway." How many times have you had to face a fear that you attempted to bury? How many times did it resurface? Do you believe that is an accident? I am terrified of snakes which I alluded to in Chapter 1. But more than that I am horror-struck at the thought of drowning, being in water without a safety net, so to speak. I am about to share with you how my faith was strengthened after I finally faced that reoccurring fear. The relapse of this fear took on a life of its own and challenged me with several near-death situations over a lifetime. I am excited to share with you how I took my control back from the anxiety monster and defeated my fear of drowning once and for all.

My fear of drowning began when I was eight years old during our family vacation. It was the Summer of 1985 and Sunset Beach was a pretty well-kept secret at the time. Sunset is located in Brunswick County in North Carolina not far from the South Carolina border and the only way to visit the island in those days was to cross a swing bridge. The historic pontoon bridge sprawled the intercoastal waterway and opened once an hour for all boats and anytime for commercial watercraft. We rented a modest ocean front cottage and set up our beach camp each day a few yards from the surf. There were pockets of families scattered up and down the eight mile stretch of beach. Dad was working on blowing up the Hampshire deluxe beach float that was manufactured to last forever but was not so gentle on the skin. I was attempting to body surf while I waited for the float. I had not learned to respect the current at that time and the rip tide was pulling me further and further out. Once I was past the wave's breaking point I started to float on my back, watching the passing pelican parade above me. The tide was shifty and suddenly I was unable to gain any footing. Without warning I could not touch the sandy bottom, I tried to remember my swimming strokes, but the current was too strong. I called for my parents, but they did not hear me. Waves were breaking, one after one in my face and by the time the fifth wave hit, my stamina was on its last leg. I did not have long before the remainder of my energy would give out. Suddenly, a college aged man appeared out of nowhere and pulled me to safety just in time. The memory of that day haunted me for a good fifteen years. My Dad would ask me every summer to go jet skiing with him and Kiki on the intercoastal and my response was always, "No." I could not fathom getting on a motorized device that had killed people or left them stranded and defenseless in open water, granted they were likely being reckless, but that terrifying image was enough to make my answer an easy one. It is strange really; I have had a few scary near-death water experiences over the years. Maybe God is trying to tell me something?

In the Fall of 2016, my husband Kevin and I visited Belize for the first time. Our dear friends Scott and Curt moved from Chicago to Ecuador a couple years before and we were trying to find a logical place to meet up for a visit.

We rented a stunning villa at the Muy'Ono Resort in Hopkins Bay and made plans to see several hot spots including the Belize Barrier Reef, Actun Tunichil Muknal Cave and Archaeological Reserve, and a jungle adventure in the Toledo District. I believe Scott and Curt's pictures could be found beside the definition of "adventure" in the dictionary, and their international exploits and colorful stories are legendary. When I grow up, I want to have at least a small percentage of the spunky spirit they both have for exotic travel and experience spontaneity. Oh wait, I am currently forty-four years old, so I guess that ship has sailed but I can always count on Scott and Curt, and my sweet Kevin, to encourage me to put at least my pinky toe into the water of their exciting escapades while we are together. I think that is an important indicator for a strong friendship, when the other person (or people in this case) help you to grow past your fears toward new life experiences.

Our first day trip in Belize was a guided tour by Carlos the Caveman (yes, that was his self-entitled professional name) to the deep ancient Mayan underworld located in the Actun Tunichil Muknal Cave (also known as the ATM cave.) The cave was located just over an hour from our resort, and we hired a local family to drive us to our various excursions during our ten days in Belize. When we arrived at the ATM Cave parking lot, we met Carlos who assigned cave gear to the four of us which included a hard hat, battery powered headlamp, and life vest. Carlos packed one bag with waters, first aid, and I am pretty sure I saw the glimmer of a machete that he tried to hide from plain view. Once we were geared up, we began the forty-five-minute walk through the forest. A family of monkeys whistled at us from above and the path had also been visited by Pumas earlier that day, their impressive paw prints left behind in the mud. The entrance to the ATM cave is in the shape of an hour-glass which is fitting as we would be below ground for several hours. At this point I chuckled to myself as I thought the height of the adventure was observing wild Puma prints on our hike to the cave, but boy was I wrong.

When Carlos explained we would be swimming fifteen-feet across alligator infested water into a cave where he had seen both a Viper snake and a Puma, all the color drained out of my face. Then he told us that they had been experiencing a lot of rain and one time he got trapped in the cave with a couple from Florida for several hours when the water elevated to cover the entrance passage…at which point my stomach took a nosedive. Finally, he shared we would be testing our fears of tight places and heights when we had to inch our way through the section of cave called, "the guillotine" followed by a risky climb of a twenty-foot ladder to see the Mayan skeletons…at which point I thought I might faint. But you know what? I did every bit of it, and I had fun! I almost thought I had been inducted into the Scott and Curt Adventure Club until we embarked on our trip to the Belize Barrier Reef a couple of days later.

We depended on our new friends Barbara and Elvin to secure a boat transport to visit the Belize Barrier Reef. Barbara and Elvin took us to the ATM Cave a couple of days before, and we had been invited to enjoy local grouper at her restaurant too. We probably should have been more specific about what kind of boat we wished to rent as the one waiting for us resembled a rowboat with bench style seating. The four of us boarded the "rowboat" (okay, it did have a motor but only had about a two-foot canopy which provided no shelter for us, and mild protection to the captain of the modest vessel). Scott and Curt loaded their scuba equipment while Kevin and I packed our snorkels in a cinch sack. We began the very slow trek to the Reef, and it felt like it would take us most of the day to get there as the motor appeared to be dying. The sun was beaming at us, inviting us to the water. It seemed like the perfect day to explore the Reef. We had no idea that a massive storm was brewing. Fifteen minutes into our trip, I inspected the threatening clouds over head and heard thunder in the distance. The first mate, also known as the boat driver's ten-year-old son, made quick passage to the hull where he would be protected from the storm. Twenty minutes later that fast-acting storm erupted like a sleeping volcano without warning. The captain said nothing, just focused on getting us to safety although by that point, there was no land as far as the eye could see. Imagine body crushing rain with only a towel over our heads, deep loud booming thunder, and lightning so close you could smell it. I was in my own personal hell, and I completely freaked out, crying, screaming, and shaking. My metaphoric invite to Scott and Curt's Adventure Club was soon blown away by the colossal wind and my fragile mind had become a runaway.

In moments of crisis, I usually have a waterfall of thoughts turning somersaults in my brain, it is miserable. Why did we not check the radar before boarding the boat? What if we are struck by lightning? Who will rescue us? Who will raise our seven kids? What if the boat sinks and I drown? I just wanted to turn my irrational brain off. Scott and Curt were sitting behind Kevin and me; between sobs I noticed how perfectly calm they both were. I was envious, wishing I could just shake off the feeling of terror that had taken over me in a matter of minutes. We were caught in the storm for almost an hour but thankfully the only casualty to fall from the boat that day was my cell phone. Our wonderful captain was able to get us out of danger to a nearby island and bonus, it had a festive tiki bar and a splendid beach boasting calm waves of crystal-clear Caribbean blue water. We had salvaged the day and were now enjoying rum punch, an authentic Belizean lunch, swimming and snorkeling in luminous water warmed by the shining rebounded sun. Nearby photographers were guiding Miss Belize's photo shoot on the most beautiful stretch of beach I had ever seen. My faith was not what it should have been at that time. As a practicing Christian I should have believed God would take care of us and the reminder of his promises made me feel slightly foolish as I enjoyed the remainder of the perfect sunny day. Something had to change but I was not sure where to begin.

Curt, Ally, Kevin, and Scott in Belize, 2016

My most bone chilling water scare happened in a river if you can believe it. Who could imagine that a river could hold a more terrifying story than the vastness of the sea and her impressive waves? It was the summer of 2006 and I had just given birth to my second baby a few months before. My Bible study tribe had decided to take a trip together. I referred to this group of ladies as a tribe because the anthropology of our association was linked by impactful life events that made us feel like family. Our church was very large and there were often opportunities to grow our faith with growth groups, unique travel opportunities and team building experiences in addition to church on Sunday. The six of us planned to drive to Tennessee on a Friday and ride the middle and upper Ocoee River in a white-water raft on Saturday and return home on Sunday for dinner. Our husbands stayed behind and cared for the children, and we made arrangements to stay in a nearby cabin for the two nights in Tennessee. It was a rustic accommodation of eight bunks and one bathroom. I was not a big camper but was looking forward to some quiet time with God, so the lodging really did not matter.

I guess my sleep deprived mommy brain missed the part that the competitive canoeing event for the 1996 Summer Olympics was held on the very course we would be riding on the Ocoee. The other very important part of information I missed was that six people had died on the course in less than ten years. I was just happy for some girl time; the details did not seem to matter in the moment I made the decision to go on the trip. We were all laughing and joking as we met our guide in a nearby camp area. Dave was a tall, hippy looking dude with long dirty blonde hair, Chaco's sandals, and a big invigorating smile. You could tell this was his passion, he was excited to share the Ocoee with the world, and in that moment, the six of us.

White-water rafting 101 lasted about fifteen minutes, then we signed a waiver so the rafting company could not be sued for any unforeseen accidents. We all climbed into the raft, one by one. We were instructed to anchor our feet in the creases of the raft and paddle together on cue during orientation. There was a brief mention of what to do if you ended up outside of the raft in open water. Once I had my paddle, I took my seat in the middle of the raft, on the left side between two of my tribal sisters, Melissa and Jen. I was so excited to wear my new Keens, an exciting score at the local T.J. Maxx, and practiced lodging my foot with the impressive tread into the furrow. I strapped my protective helmet on with fraying straps that were still damp from the last group. I was ready and moderately nervous, but mostly excited.

Dave pushed us off the bank and we ventured down the river, the sun peaking in at us through the trees. We were surrounded by the Cherokee National Forest and the views were breath taking. We were all dressed in athletic shorts and tank tops, over-sized life jackets, and bright yellow helmets. We started to descend the river and the water current picked up. It was a very warm day in May and the splash of the river water over the side of the raft was a refreshing delight on our exposed legs. The Ocoee was very busy that day and more than twenty rafting companies had assigned passengers to multiple rafts. We were approaching the first rapids, "the Mikey's" and our guide told us to brace ourselves as our raft charged the first two drops. We all cheered as the boat leveled off, and I felt elated, loosening the white-knuckle grip on my paddle. This was supposed to be fun and even though I was initially nervous, I was determined to suck every bit of the juice out of the over-ripened experience. It was deep, fast-moving, unpredictable water but also a coming-of-age experience I had always wanted to try. What could happen, I was with my tribe and Dave and surely nothing could go wrong. Those are always our famous last words, and ones we often come to regret.

As we approached the Olympic course my heart began to beat loudly, booming like a tympani drum in my ears. I looked up to see a large suspension bridge and took a deep breath and dug my foot in deeper. Dave told us when we saw the bridge, we needed to be ready. We were about to battle class 111 and IV rapids, which equals huge drops and big waves. Some of these rapids have very telling names: "Grumpy," "Table Saw," "Broken Nose," and "Hell Hole." Once we entered the Olympic course it all became a blur and soon it became clear why the rapids had been given the hair-raising, actually, hair-drenching labels but wait, I am getting ahead of myself. The raft was being tossed back and forth in the massive waves. Dave's voice was lost in the roar of the waterfall. We struggled to dig our paddles into rushing water, and my stomach had taken a trip of its own and was now in my throat. We turned a corner and there were boats everywhere, a traffic jam of sorts and we were headed for a colossal drop. We were not aligned for this drop and everyone could hear and feel the fear in Dave's voice as he yelled for us to brace and lean forward. The raft hit hard at the bottom of the rapid, we were dangerously close to "Hell Hole." If you fall out of the boat and get stuck in a whirlpool-rapid (like Hell Hole) you must tuck yourself into a ball and allow the hole to catapult you out. Visualize a circus cannon shooting out an ambitious performer.

When we hit bottom, my body was like a sling shot and suddenly I was in the turbulent water. Not only was I in the water, but I was also stuck under our raft. I kicked and fought, losing one of my new shoes forever to the Ocoee. I was struggling with asthma that year and began to panic knowing my lungs were ill equipped to handle such an ordeal. I swam like hell, moving my raw-stunned cold arms and legs against the violent current. My head finally breached, and I was above the water. The scene above water; however, was not much better. Pandemonium had a new meaning and image that day. I searched and searched for my tribe and the raft. They were several yards away waiting for me in the raft, secured to the overcrowded bank of the river. Dave threw me a line, but it took several throws for me to catch it, as I tried to tread water and keep my head above the relentless tidal motion of the stream.

Dave finally pulled me to the raft. As he pulled me up into the raft, I mooned all the spectators, as the "man" over-board accident had now become crowd-view worthy. I felt like the main character in a cheesy horror film that new actresses sign with a brief nudity commitment to secure their initial spot in Hollywood. My carefully tied shorts had slipped off my hips as my body slumped over the side of the raft, defeated after the fight with the uncompromising river current that felt like my worst enemy. Did I mention this all happened directly below the observation deck that was populated with almost one hundred people? It really did not matter; I was too exhausted to care. My tribe looked at me in horror, my lips blue and face, white as a ghost. If I could have grown wings and flown out of there, I would have. Sadly, the scary adventure was not over, and I had to pull it together to continue, and with only one shoe. How would I anchor myself with one shoe? I felt emotionally fractured as I came to the realization that I had just experienced another almost drowning. The only thing I could think to do was pray. Not only did I pray, but I also repeated the same verse over and over in my head. *I can do all things through Christ who strengthens me. I can do all things through Christ who strengthens me. I can do all things through Christ who strengthens me.* (Philippians 4:13) The verse became my mantra and after a few minutes I felt calmer, and my heartbeat slowed down and was less frantic.

The phrase "fear not" is used 365 times in the Bible. Can you believe that? Clearly, God does not want us to be fearful. This was impossibly difficult for me, as I survived three terrifying water incidents. How could I not be scared? I was missing a key point, *I survived!* Once I fully comprehended that God was trying to send me a message, I studied fear further. Joshua 1:9 tells us, "Have I not commanded you? Be strong and courageous! Do not tremble or be dismayed, for the Lord your God is with you wherever you go." God was with me! I was not alone! Right then and there I decided part of my process for approaching potentially stressful situations would involve engaging in a prayer mantra. I would say it repeatedly when feeling overwhelmed. Has this happened to you, my friend? Have you been scared about a situation or event? Do you feel the weight of the fear heavy on your mind and heart? What would it feel like to face and conquer that fear once and for all? Well, I can tell you. As I said, I developed a prayer mantra and became mindful of the many opportunities in my life where I could utilize it. The funny thing is that I began the prayer mantra more than eight years before that trip to Belize, when I was on the Ocoee River, yet I did not use that tool when we were stuck in the rowboat in the storm. I had all the tools I needed to trust that God and our rowboat captain would bring us to safety that day but somewhere along the way, I forgot how to use them. I think my fear triggered the trauma of hidden memories of that river accident until recently. God knew exactly when to remind me of the prayer mantra tool right before a recent trip with my husband.

One year ago, right before the pandemic hit, my husband took me to Key West for a long weekend. We were tired of the Virginia winter and were craving warm weather and sun! When we arrived, we did some exploring near the marina and Kevin asked me if I wanted to take a jet ski tour around the Keys? My heart skipped a beat as I recalled the many times my Dad had invited me to go jet skiing and I was right back in freak out mode subconsciously. I tried to make other suggestions but wanted to make him happy as he always compromised with activities I wanted to do. This was my chance, time to put my money where my mouth was regarding facing my fears. I said yes and with a smile on my face. We headed out on the jet ski with our guide, McKenzie.

Kevin drove the jet ski and I held on to his waist behind him. It was a challenge to drive as the water was rough, and the ocean littered with various watercraft. We got into a rhythm and I was so excited to see house boats, sandbars, and colorful fish. We were close to the reef and the water was very shallow. The water current got even more choppy the farther out we were, and I felt myself beginning to worry. Immediately I began my prayer mantra, trying to focus on being calm. *I can do all things through Christ who strengthens me. I can do all things through Christ who strengthens me. I can do all things through Christ who strengthens me.* In a flash and without warning the jet ski flipped, violently dropping Kevin and me into the warm Florida water. It felt like I had taken a neti pot treatment without reading the directions, and as I resurfaced from the water it took me a minute to get my bearings. Kevin was panicked as he thought I had hit my head in the accident that was now attracting attention from other boaters. I was fine. More than fine actually, the thing I was worried about (falling off the jet ski) had happened and I was ok! It was a life changing realization. God had shown me how to conquer the fear and I felt powerful and confident.

I was 43 years old and had lived decades fearing the very thing that makes up 60% of our bodies, water. I grew up swimming and although I was no Katie Ledecky, I was a decent swimmer. So why did I fear water and drowning so much? As I mentioned before, fear is talked about a lot in the Bible. My conclusion for my fear of water; my relationship with God needed work. This is where the morning routine pops up again. Getting centered with prayer before you start your day is important; however, equally imperative is praying before you engage in that activity that has you frightened. The combination of the preliminary prayer and the prayer mantra during the event broke the fear barrier for me. It was almost as if I were putting on a second life preserver, and although you could not see it, I was fully protected. Life is too short to sit on the sidelines, watching strangers live the life you are fully capable of living. It is time to strap yourself to that metaphoric bungee apparatus and get ready to jump to freedom from your current fears.

LIFE LESSON #6
Conquer your fears and develop a prayer
mantra.

I believe it is very common to run from, avoid, and reject activities that scare us. I did this for years, twenty-plus years to be exact. It feels like you are constantly gripping the "oh crap" handle in your car which does not allow you to go very far. When we allow ourselves to grow out of our comfort zone amazing things start to happen. Because I took the plunge and faced my fear, I am now closer than ever to God. I trust him, I believe he will take care of me and my loved ones. All of this was born out of the biblical study of fear and developing my prayer mantra. You can do this too, my sister! You can do anything you set your mind to. I believe in your ability to vanquish your fear and become the courageous person God wants you to be.

In case you are looking for ideas to develop your own mantra please find some suggestions below, some are biblical and some merely inspirational.

*   *   *   *

"Be strong and courageous; do not be frightened and do not be dismayed, for the Lord your God is with you wherever you go." Joshua 1:9

"Surely God is my salvation; I will trust and not be afraid. The Lord, the Lord, is my strength and my song; he has become my salvation." Isaiah 12:2

"My flesh and my heart may fail, but God is the strength of my heart and my portion forever." Psalm 73:26

"But the Lord is faithful, and he will strengthen you and protect you from the evil one." 2 Thessalonians 3:3

"You cannot swim for new horizons until you have courage to lose sight of the shore." William Faulkner

"Courage is an inner resolution to go forward despite obstacles." Martin Luther King, Jr.

"You never know how strong you are until being strong is the only choice you have." Cayla Mills

"The world breaks everyone, and afterward, some are strong at the broken places." Ernest Hemingway

CHAPTER 7
TEAM EDWARD

On October 1, 2010, I left my first husband. I carefully planned my exit from our marriage for months. I wrote him a letter and grieved the end of the marriage in that final week. I took my engagement and wedding rings off my finger, revealing the reminder of our Indian Summer and the white stripe that had not seen the light of day in over seven years. It was a Friday and only my parents knew of my plan to leave him. He left for work at 7:30 a.m. and did not know that in a matter of hours my two little angels and I would be gone and would never return to the life that we lived, the four of us.

Do you remember *The Twilight Saga*, a collection of four novels about vampires and wolves that also were made into movies? Oh, how I resisted reading these books, I protested they were cheesy and predictable, and finally I gave in and I was wrong about all of it. The summer before we left, I caved and began reading the first, second and then all the books. I was mesmerized, drinking in every detail of the destination, the characters, and the love story. My sweet children were in

Vacation Bible School one week of the summer. I spent that entire week, barricaded in Starbucks, and read every single book, cover to cover while sipping iced vanilla lattes. The love story was like oxygen, and my personal existence was on life support. I found myself enchanted by Edward and Bella's love story. An impossible love, divided by complicated biology and immortality. When the *Twilight* movies came out my entrancement became amplified as I fixated on their perfect chemistry on the screen. I realized it was fiction, but something about that series was deeply spiritual for me and touched my heart. When Edward says, "Her existence alone was excuse enough to justify the creation of the entire world," I was swept off my feet. I was enthralled by Edward's heroic character and the depth of love he displayed for Bella. It reminded me of my parent's marriage, and it was painfully obvious that my marriage was the opposite.

I escaped to the theater to see the second *Twilight* movie, New Moon alone. I daydreamed, with tear-stained cheeks, of a true love where two souls are intertwined in such a way that their entire world becomes each other. You find it difficult to breathe without the other person and cannot get enough of their company. Even your worst day is livable because they are beside you, holding your hand and your heart. Your trust in their genuine character and the loving relationship you have designed, symbolized by impenetrable steel that cannot be destroyed by the outside world. Your passion for their body and soul can never be satisfied. You relentlessly crave intimacy and becoming one. They are unapologetically romantic and look for opportunities to make you smile. They are caring, kind, and gentle with your family. And when you meet that person, for the very first time, you feel fireworks in your pulse and warm red rapture in your beaming smile. Suddenly you know you have met "the one."

The day I decided to leave my husband had been carefully planned for over a month. His relentless negativity had escalated to unresolved anger and his reoccurring role of playing the victim had become permanent and the entire family was being pulled into the drama. I never told him I was leaving; I just left a letter on the kitchen counter explaining my actions. My parents arrived at 10:00 a.m. and we began packing two cars with mine and the kids' clothing, toiletries, and a few toys. My Mom and Dad had come to my rescue again, offering a consoling haven while I figured out my next step. The four of us had been living in Mooresville, North Carolina at the time and I was able to secure permission to move back to Blacksburg, Virginia from a North Carolina Judge.

The first four months in Blacksburg were tough. I could not find a job as the employment pool was shallow and I had been teaching music and singing with Opera Carolina for the last five years. I applied for countless jobs, many of which I was not qualified for. Nevertheless, I kept trying and in my free time I walked the Huckleberry Trail. I prayed and walked, miles and miles, it was my therapy and God, the therapist. My four-year old son was in pre-school and my five-year-old daughter was in kindergarten in the same elementary school I attended. Walking the halls of the Margaret Beeks Elementary School saturated my mind with memories of cupcake days, book fairs, and square dances in homemade costumes in the early 80s. Never in my wildest dreams did I think I would be living in my hometown again, and as a single mom. I felt like a failure as I was definitely the minority as a spouseless parent in Blacksburg at that time. The exchange with other parents did not always feel hospitable and it was obvious that a couple of moms in the mix saw me as a dangerous threat. This had everything to do with them going through the motions of a bad marriage, much like I had experienced myself, but not being ready to take the chance that a happier life was possible. Little did they know that half of them would be divorced or separated by the time our kids walked the stage at 5th grade graduation. It was a lonely beginning but both kids were making friends and seemed happy, and their laughter and smiles were medicine for my soul.

One helpful piece of information I collected during my taxing quest to find a job: it is all about who you know. Allow me to introduce you to my two saviors, Elaine and Krisha. I will tell you about Krisha shortly, but let us begin with Elaine. I actually already told you about Elaine in Chapter 4, my "mother" boss at the opera company in Washington, D.C. Elaine and I had lost touch after I moved to North Carolina; I had not spoken to her in over five years. Once we relocated to Lake Norman, I lost touch with just about everyone I knew in D.C. Then I joined Facebook, albeit a bit late, and the reunions began with friend requests and direct messages. I worked for Elaine for six years while in Washington and in that time, I determined she was the classiest person I had ever known. She could hold a conversation with anyone in the room, be it a Supreme Court Justice or the custodian emptying her office trash. She treated everyone with respect, and I always looked to her like a mother figure. I reconnected with Elaine on Facebook and shared the details of the dissolution of my marriage and our recent move to Blacksburg. Elaine offered to write me a recommendation and permitted me to use it for every single application and interview. As a highly esteemed music professor at Catholic University, her recommendation would carry a lot of weight in the collegiate community of Blacksburg and Virginia Tech. This was not just any recommendation; it was the kindest letter I have ever read and likely one of the two missing pieces to my future success in Virginia. The second being the introduction Krisha provided, but more on this later. Elaine and I remain in touch, and I will forever be grateful for her support and assistance in one of the darkest hours of my life.

I turned thirty-four roughly six weeks after we moved. Ever since I beat cancer, birthdays were very important to me in my quest to take nothing for granted. For the last several years it was just me and the kids celebrating a quiet birthday. My husband always chose to go on an annual boy's sailing trip on my birthday weekend. It was hurtful but I became indifferent, burying my feelings as I had done hundreds of times when he chose other people over me. Not this year, however, this year I was free as a bird and my childhood friend, Krisha, had planned a dinner party for me at my favorite restaurant, Cabo Fish Taco. I pulled out a black cocktail dress from the back of the closet and dusted off my red pumps that I had not put on since my honeymoon. Krisha and five of her friends reserved a table in the front of the restaurant. We enjoyed Mahi tacos, queso and chips and pomegranate margaritas. The conversation felt like an endless spool of velvet ribbon, decorated with fascinating stories and exuberant laughter. How lavish to enjoy an entire day with no agenda but to have fun and celebrate. I had not had an adult dinner in years and did not want the night to end. It was a perfect birthday, and I was beginning to feel like the woman I used to know.

Krisha and I have been friends since we were toddlers. She has caring brown eyes and beautiful long jet-black hair; her appearance is always flawless with colorful outfits and stunning make-up. Her nails are always painted, and the theme typically pays homage to one of the exotic locales she has visited in her travels. She is a local celebrity but manages to make time for everyone she runs into no matter their rank in her life. Krisha's parents are immigrants from India, and I remember her sharing their beautiful story at a local women's leadership event a couple of years ago. Krisha's parents, like mine, had worked hard for every piece of their success and sharing that inspiring history brought us even closer together as friends. Our mothers met (as did we) in the Montessori School we attended in a local church. I remember dressing up in unique Halloween costumes each year with Krisha for school parties. We were also giddy with elation to don frilly dresses in November and January for each of our birthday parties at the local Burger King. Yep, you read that right…it was the 80s and event venues were limited, actually non-existent, in rural Virginia. Thankfully, we made up for it in our young adult years as we both lived exciting lives, and frequented fancy (and sometimes not fancy) bars in our twenties in Washington, D.C. In the fall of 2010, fate had found us both back in Blacksburg at the same time and she included me on invitations to happy hours, karaoke nights, dinner parties and her signature monthly networking event, "Up on the Roof," that she had designed and operated for over a decade. Krisha was selfless in her pursuit to help Blacksburg High School graduates create relevant and happy lives as returning adults in Blacksburg. I was thankful for her tenacity as my career opportunities seemed bleak and my attitude was becoming more and more sour each day.

The fourth month of living at home with my parents was rounding to a close and the job search felt hopeless, a big black hole of nothing. I was wearing down and I could tell we had out stayed our welcome as my son had broken one of my Mom's knick-knacks at least once a week. One evening I was in the pediatrician's office; both kids had strep throat. I was exhausted mentally and physically, wondering how I would pay for their medication as I only had twenty dollars left in my checking account. I was too prideful to ask my husband for the child support that was still being calculated. The day before I had caused a mild car accident, trying to help the kids with a snack, and now had two car repairs on the horizon. I wondered when I would ever be able to find my smile again with all this pressure that was looming and no solution in sight. The doctor left the room, leaving the door a jar. As I waited for him to return with the prescription slip, I studied the innocent faces of my precious children while silently thanking God for the spectacular gift of being their mom. Without warning something remarkable happened. Miraculously a text from Krisha chimed in just as the doctor left the room. In her text was a gift, and one I desperately needed, a legitimate job lead! God knew what I needed as I sat downhearted in the waiting room with my sick children, and suddenly it was as if a butterfly had flown through the open door, signifying undeniable hope. Krisha was a proven mover and shaker and her social calendar had entertained a conversation with a local attorney who was looking for some customer service assistance in his firm. Two days later I interviewed and was offered the job, Client Services Director for a local intellectual property law firm. What does that have to do with music you might ask? Nothing. But that was okay! I had a job, and I was finally able to take care of my babies, pay my bills, and I felt confident I made the right decision to move home.

Ally & Krisha
Burger King, 1982

Krisha & Ally,
UOTR Gala, 2012

When you are the Client Services Director for a law firm you do a lot of networking. I attended breakfast meetings, lunch and learns, and after-hours events. I was so thankful I stayed home with my children during the day the first five years of their lives; I'd worked nights teaching and singing in North Carolina. This new season of my life, and with the kids in school, meant we had less time together. It was a difficult adjustment at first, but I knew in my heart I had done the right thing. Within six months the growing pains of our new life were beginning to subside, and I had never been happier. We were also able to get our own place and start writing a new story, just the three of us.

A couple of months after starting the new job at the law firm I attended a Chamber of Commerce networking event. The venue was a historic farmhouse appropriately named the "Farmhouse," and the charming locale was built in the 1800's. I had been to the Farmhouse a handful of times as a child. Dad always took us there to celebrate various occasions. I can still recall sitting in the dimly lit booth enjoying their famous onion rings and a Shirley Temple mocktail. Kiki and I felt so grown up as it was usually the setting for milestones like engagement proposals or retirement parties. I entered the wood paneled entry way, and suddenly I was ten years old again. The same antique pitcher sat on the hostess stand filled to the brim with fragments of old-time peppermint sticks and the aroma of prime rib tickled my nostrils as I made my way to the event room. It was a chilly February night, but the crackling fire warmed my frozen skin as I accepted a glass of red wine from the bartender. I cannot explain it but the day and, more specifically, that event felt like it was earmarked for something transformative. Little did I know I was on the precipice of discovering the life I had always dreamed of.

Out of the corner of my eye I saw Krisha a few feet away. We had planned to meet up and mingle at the event together. Krisha was talking to a handsome, dark haired man with a smile that made me go weak in the knees. He was casually dressed in a yellow t-shirt, golf shorts, and he had several rubber bracelets on his arm signifying the local charities he was supporting. I felt my heart flutter as he shook my hand, while Krisha carefully crafted a thoughtful introduction that I only half listened to. I was mesmerized by his quiet confidence and natural charisma. I felt as though there was a spotlight on the two of us and no one else was in the room. He had an unmistakable "je ne sais quoi" and his alluring x factor had piqued my interest. Krisha and I graduated high school together and she knew everyone in town, holding a highly respected town council position. Krisha has too many talents to list but the one she is most proficient at is being an expert connector. Krisha is the one who made it possible for me to finally gain meaningful employment, and now a man?!? Krisha was soon pulled away by a resident following up on an important town issue but not before suggesting I share with Kevin our impressive business law offerings at the firm.

Kevin is a born leader and successful entrepreneur. He shared with me that he was a Domino's Pizza franchisee, owning several locations in the New River Valley and Roanoke. The sincerity of his gaze, and perfect eye contact made me nervous. He was fully in the moment, not half listening to what I was saying which was a new experience for me. I had become a highly functioning introvert in just a couple of months; however, had spent the last ten years conversing with mostly young humans at work. It was only my second appearance at a business event, and my obvious neglect of adult conversation meant, I put my foot in my mouth, a lot! My response to Kevin: "I like Papa John's pizza better." In what universe do you tell the boy you kind of like that you prefer his competitor's product more than his. Did I mention I had not flirted with anyone in ten years? Kevin grinned and giggled without prejudice, and I was relieved our conversation had not missed a beat. I was so thankful my crush translated my sassy moxie as endearing instead of obnoxious. Better than that, Kevin loved a challenge! Our effortless conversation continued from work to kids to the discovery that we were both in the middle of divorce proceedings. I believe that God was flashing the big green blinking arrow in that moment but there was no time to see it as I had to rush out to relieve the babysitter. Our parting that night was bittersweet as there was no plan to see each other, just a traditional exchange of business cards that was customary at those events. I hopped in the frigid car with a shiver that traveled my entire body, wondering if and when I would ever see this fascinating man again.

In the Intro of this book, I talked about the existence of afterglow. In my humble opinion there is no brighter afterglow than the one that comes after you meet the love of your life. This is especially true after you have had the door slammed in your face multiple times from unrequited affection either personally or professionally. The afterglow I felt that first night after meeting Kevin was an exhilaration that is difficult to put into words. It made me feel shiny all over, covered in perpetual sparkle. It would not rub or wash off. It was constant. The feeling was like a drug and even affected my love and expression of fashion, which has always been my addiction of choice. The afterglow of meeting Kevin forever attracted me to all things that shine. I became obsessed with the idea of displaying the inner glimmer I felt, on the outside. If you look in my closet, you will a lot of sparkle... sequins, beading, glitter on jackets, skirts, dresses and even shoes! This signature style inspired by my brightest afterglow moment is another testament to hope and the creative ways we can display our positivity. My glitzy symbol of pure jubilation reminds me to stay the course because beyond our worst days is the promise that the sun will rise again, warmer, and more lustrous than ever. Life is short, always take time to sparkle and shine and if your luminosity is too much for spectators, that is their problem, not yours!

* * * *

Life is short, always take time to sparkle and shine and if your luminosity is too much for spectators, that is their problem, not yours!

* * * *

I mentioned Kevin loves a challenge—he is also the most romantic man I have ever known. He was determined to change my mind about Papa John's and sent a large selection of his pizza, to my office the next day, determined to make me a Domino's Pizza lover. My co-workers teased me while devouring the pizzas. It was a good day at work, and he had made me the hero with my team. I called to thank him, shared that I loved the thin crust Pacific veggie pizza, and we made plans for our next rendezvous. Kevin's romantic gesture with the pizza party had overshadowed Eric's red rose and, in a flash, I had hope again that true love was possible more than once in a lifetime. Who would have thought it possible, but again, God always has a plan.

Two days later Kevin arrived at my home for our first official date. I had recently moved into my new home. I was so proud of my little white house. I called it the four-door house as there were four exterior doors which seemed odd for a 1500 square foot home. It was a 1920s Cape Cod style house complete with a second story loft that the kids used for a playroom. There was a music room for my piano and a dining nook where the three of us ate, around the table, as a family. There was a fenced in yard where we played soccer while dodging skunk holes. Yes, we had a skunk problem but no matter, I had done the impossible, I was raising my kids in a beautiful home all on my own! Never in my wildest dreams did I think I could do it and only five months after leaving my husband. Kevin entered the side door into my family room with an Iron Man gift bag in his hand, a house-warming gift to celebrate the new house. Inside the bag was a collection of wine accessories, including an assortment of rubber corks and a black and chrome wine opener. I took my cue and opened a bottle of red wine with my new gift and joined him on the sofa. I kissed Kevin on the cheek to thank him for the thoughtful gift, without warning his face pivoted and his full lips met mine. I plunged, without a life raft, into the most delicious, breathless, seductive kiss of my life and I was a goner. The depth of that kiss made my head swim in the luscious current of sensuality which started at my lips, eventually sending electric current down my spine and legs to the end of my toes. It was a full body seize and I was finally a casualty of true love.

Kevin and I dated for the next two years, and it was bliss. He reminded me of my Daddy. He had grown up in a modest home not far from where both of my parents grew up in Roanoke, Virginia. My Daddy was a self-made man, a caring doctor, and every piece of his success was earned through blood, sweat and tears. I saw the same raw determination in Kevin. He took a risk and did not go to college. He chose to begin a management career at age nineteen with Domino's. He worked hard, and quickly it became clear that he was, and always would be, the hardest worker in the room. He inspires me every day with his work ethic, passion, and natural leadership ability.

As we got to know each other I began to check must haves off my "soul mate list." Kevin was very magnanimous, donating time, pizza, and money to local causes that included kids and families in need. Kevin is generous and a community advocate, check! He did not play games, Kevin called when he said he would and texted me all the time. Kevin is not a player, check! When he looked at me, I felt like the only woman in the room, and he always put me first. Kevin appears to be smitten with me, check! Kevin was caring and considerate of my children, and he has five daughters of his own. Kevin loves children, check! I remember how nervous he was to tell me; little did he know it was my dream to have a big family. Kevin would come to see me almost every day and I did not mind; I could not get enough of his company. We enjoy spending a lot of time together, check!

Kevin had also experienced more than his share of adversity, losing his Dad at age eleven. The trauma of losing a parent would leave other men paralyzed but Kevin allowed it to direct him into a clear purpose like a slingshot. He became a mentor to others who had lost parents, a role model who had come out on the other side of unimaginable suffering a stronger, more focused man. The focus always being all the good things happening in life, an important reminder to me who still felt the occasional pull from the demons of my past. I had spent years living in negativity caused by my own adversity, married to a man who was convinced that the world was against him. Kevin pulled me into the light, saving me from the demise that was certainly my future had I stayed in my marriage.

Ally & Kevin volunteering, 2011   *Kevin & Ally, Leadership NRV, 2011*

One-night as spring was beginning to blossom Kevin and I sat in rocking chairs, sipping red wine on my side porch. I had just put the kids to bed, and we were enjoying a quiet moment. Kevin took my hand, my body trembled, responding to the warmth of his touch. He suggested we play the question game that night, engaging in a survey of lesser-known information about each other. *What is your favorite color? What was the first band you saw in concert? What is your favorite movie? What is your middle name?*

I shared my middle name was "Raines" and that it was a family name, not a spaced-out hippy's decision on a whim. He chuckled and paused for a moment before answering the same question: "My middle name is Edward." My heart skipped a beat and I almost choked on my wine. It was as if God had just hit me with the last snowball of winter, delivering a promise, a gift, that the happy season of spring and a fresh start at life (and love) was upon me. All those months I had spent investigating all the angles of the *Twilight* love story, and what felt like an obsession had actually been a sign from God. I was too broken from a bad marriage to believe I deserved more during the summer of *Twilight*, but God's promises do not have an expiration date. I knew, in that very moment, I had found "the one" and the person God had intended me to love. The cold winter I had endured for seven years with my first husband was melting away and I had hope again. I snickered to myself and thought, well played, God, well played. God had intervened, I was in heaven, in the arms of a man who truly loved me, and I deeply loved him.

In May of 2013 we were married with all seven of our children, our parents, and our sisters in attendance. I wore a floor-length strapless white dress with cascading delicate ruffles, accented with a satin beaded sash. Kevin and my son wore matching khaki day tuxedos. Our girls wore matching peach dresses with ivory patent leather Mary Janes. All of us had a special role and having all of our children participate created a perfect ceremony and start to our lives together. We chose the song, "A Thousand Years," as it was the love song from *Twilight's Breaking Dawn*. It was played by a solo violinist and as she transitioned to the chorus with a fantastic crescendo, I felt my body come alive with warmth. I imagined God was hugging me again, just like he did on my final blood transfusion during chemo, celebrating the promise he had been hinting at for years. I felt like it had taken me a thousand years to find Kevin, but our wedding day had finally arrived. We exchanged vows and committed to love each other forever, and I never looked back. A new family of nine was conceived that day and I never imagined I would ever be this happy.

We celebrated our 7th wedding anniversary a couple of months ago with a very special trip to Sunset Beach. I made the enthusiastic introduction to Kevin five years before, and he soon was swept away by my beloved place. The place I had treasured since I was six years old. The tourist season had not yet begun when I took Kevin to Sunset Beach that first March. The anniversary trip fell just under a week before tourists would be arriving for the kickoff weekend of summer and Memorial Day. We awoke just before dawn, laced up our Nikes and began the short seven-minute walk to the public access point. The sun broke dawn to reveal four shrimp boats taking their posts on the edge of the horizon. Each crew waited patiently with a chatty group of seagulls, all hoping to receive a piece of the ocean's bounty. The off season at Sunset Beach is a gift because the beach is deserted apart from a handful of year-round residents and their happy go lucky dogs who run the shore, chasing balls in the surf.

A couple years ago Nicolas Sparks wrote "Every Breath," delivering the heartfelt love story of Tru and Hope, inspired by a mailbox that produced magic. That book is based on a true story of love that started at Sunset Beach. The magical mailbox, named Kindred Spirit mailbox, lives on Bird Island, a remote stretch of beach past the 40th street access on the west end of Sunset Beach. The mailbox shares company with a rustic bench, where visitors perch, contemplating their hearts. The mailbox contains paper and pens, and the thoughts, wishes, dreams, prayers, and pain of strangers. When Eric died, I wrote a letter to him, I poured out my tormented soul and left it for the mailbox. I prayed God would tell him what he had meant to my life.

I had not touched the sea kissed metal of the black mailbox in seventeen years. On that quiet May morning, on our 7th wedding anniversary, Kevin and I made the thirty-minute trek to Kindred Spirit, love letters in hand, an offering for the cherished mailbox. A testament to our love is that we both decided to write letters to each other to offer to the mailbox. It was not planned and we both reveled at the chance decision to write the letters unbeknownst to the other. The day of our anniversary we each opened the two letters (each had a duplicate) with the intention to make the walk to Kindred Spirit. My letter for Kevin, a thank you note to God, for making all my dreams come true. Kevin continues to make all the desires of my heart come true as we are able to travel to Sunset Beach once a month these days. My heart sings a jubilant melody as we walk hand in hand, on the sand, taking in the breathtaking sunset for which the island was named. When I cross the bridge to Sunset Beach my blood pressure drops and I feel like I am home, showing up as the best possible version of myself. Kevin and I have nurtured our relationship in this special place while hunting for sand dollars, throwing the tennis ball for our dog Maggie, and observing wildlife like sting rays, turtles and even sharks. Our children have grown up loving Sunset just as I did. God made possible the miracle of the true love I found with Kevin. Kevin loved me back to life and his love allowed me to believe in fairytales again— except this time, I was marrying my king and was given the gift of five princesses. Anything is possible, my friend, take that leap of faith and never look back. God always has a plan, and my plan turned out to be even more fantastic than my wildest dreams had imagined. Remain faithful, my friend. Miracles are possible.

Ally & Kevin, Vegas Engagement, 2012

Ally & Kevin, Wedding Day, 2013

Happy 7th Anniversary to my true love, my soul mate, my kindred spirit. I love you, K!

My first visit to Sunset Beach was when I was six years old. My family has visited every year since, for a total of thirty-seven years. Sunset Beach lives in the biggest part of my heart and my soul is most alive when I walk the soft sandy coastline toward Bird Island, and the Kindred Spirit Mailbox. In those thirty-seven years I experienced loss, heartbreak, and adversity that almost broke me several times. At age twenty I battled a very aggressive cancer at my home in Virginia. During chemotherapy I dreamed of Sunset Beach. I closed my eyes and imagined the warm salty breeze on my face and the distant crashing waves at low tide. When my first marriage ended and all that remained was a shattered shell of a woman, I began praying for my kindred spirit to reveal himself. The person who truly "gets me," the person who loves me for who I am, the good and flawed.

I met you on February 17, 2011. Our eyes met across a crowded business event. I knew immediately there was something special about you. The kindness in your eyes, the warmth of your handshake when we were introduced, and the exhilarating conversation that flowed effortlessly. I do not ever remember smiling previously as much as I did that first night we met. The next day you swept me off my feet with a surprise delivery of my favorite food to my office. The next week we shared our first kiss, and it was magic. Like fairytale, tingling toes, and flushed face kind of magic. You make me feel like the only woman in the room. You tell me I am beautiful when I feel less than. You tell me you love me all the time and, in your arms, I am home and safe. You are unapologetically romantic and unconditionally generous. You answered every prayer I vented over twenty years of walking Sunset Beach, patiently asking God to put you in my path. You asked me to marry you at "the Eiffel Tower" in Las Vegas, overlooking the Bellagio Fountain Show. It was the most romantic evening of my entire life.

We were married on May 24, 2013. That was the day you gave me the world. You gave me the happiest life I could ever dream of having. You gave me thousands of glowing mornings, waking up beside my best friend. You gave me five amazing daughters who I love as my own. I gave you a young son and sweet daughter who deeply needed the love of a Daddy. Our blended family of seven makes me so happy—even when our home is loud, messy, and chaotic I would not change a thing. You gave me the ability to travel all over the world, and you showed me places that had only lived in my dreams. We captured passion in the treasured moments spent in the Caribbean, Barcelona, Paris, and our beloved Sunset Beach. You gave me a career I truly love and the ability to make a difference in the communities we serve. I continue to fall in love with you over and over again, celebrating life, with champagne and sunsets.

You gave me Sunset Beach and the ability to visit her often. Sunset Beach is our sanctuary, a greenhouse where our love can continue to grow and blossom. You make me want to be a better wife, mother, and partner and my sincere vow is to be better each day in how I love and cherish you and our family.

All my love, A

LIFE LESSON #7

Do not underestimate the existence of signs
which likely will lead you to step outside of
your comfort zone.

I have found my soul mate, the love of my life, my protector, my perfect lover, and my best friend in Kevin Edward Shaw. God brought my fairy tale to life and now I wholeheartedly believe in miracles, magic, signs, and that anything is possible if you are brave enough to take a chance. I believe God was sending me messages for years, but I was scared and unwilling to accept that God would be leading me toward divorce. It also seemed impossible that there could be a deeper meaning and hidden message in a fiction series that engrossed the few moments of my free time. My self-esteem and confidence had been cut down to nothing, I believed that I deserved to be with a man who did not know how to love me. Leaving my husband, moving home, and starting a new career were all out of my comfort zone. I had to actively pray through situations, like living on a limited budget with two growing children or learning to work in a career that I knew little about. I had to learn to co-parent with my ex and leave my grievances in the past. I had to take a risk, be vulnerable and be open to love again. I had to trust that God was in control, and he would take care of me and my children. I believed I would be punished for divorcing my husband, but God knew I was destined to be living a different life. Taking risks is not in my wheelhouse especially with my two angels in tow. I had always been a *play it safe* kind of gal and it took a lot for me to leave. I am so thankful that I took the risk, that walk of faith allowed me to find my perfect life. What are you doing today, my friend, to find yours?

CHAPTER 8
JUST BREATHE

It was the final hour in our three-and-a-half-hour bus ride from Milan to Venice. It was January in Italy; a fluffy layer of snow covered the grass, and the road was painted in an icy glaze. I cannot remember ever feeling that cold. Shivering from head to toe I tied my emerald overcoat tighter, the faux fur now tickling my neck as the heat kicked on above me. I had been given the gift of travel, and better yet, I was earning college credit for the month I was spending in Italy. I found myself daydreaming about the previous night, a bucket list moment that I was enthusiastically checking off. We arrived at La Scala opera house, and I felt like Julia Roberts in *Pretty Woman*. All my senses were engaged by the magic that was all around me. I could hear the orchestra warming up, fresh espresso being brewed at the concession kiosk, and the gorgeous gold and burgundy theatre was the perfect setting for the enchantment that would take the stage in just a few minutes. An attractive Italian usher offered his hand to escort me to my seat and I felt my face come alive as I blushed. His charm was obvious and well-practiced. There is a reason why "Casanova" is an Italian term, based on an historic Italian man. Italian men, young and old, are aficionados at flirtation and seduction. Well, at least that had been my experience in the couple of weeks I had been a visitor in Italy. As I took my seat in the grand hall, I remember feeling like a kid at Christmas as the burgundy velvet curtain opened, and the maestro signaled the orchestra. That was the night I fell in love with French opera as I watched the impressive cast deliver Donizetti's "La Fille Du Regiment." I closed my eyes and could almost hear the music again and then suddenly the bus began to slide on the ice.

The bus driver began to panic, losing control of the death trap on wheels, and bellowed, "Mamma Mia, Mamma Mia!" I could feel the pangs of fear welling up in my throat as my stomach began to turn. I looked out the window and nothing could prepare me for what I saw. A fresh accident, a car missing a windshield and badly dented and scratched on all sides was overturned and abandoned a few feet ahead. The road curved to reveal a deadly scene, and unlike a horror movie I could not turn it off. I saw a young woman in the snow with fragments of glass all around her. Her body had been lacerated above her belly button as she was thrown from the driver's seat through the windshield. Her body lay in several pieces, covered in blood that soaked the newly fallen snow. I was in shock; I could not make sense of what I saw. *Who was this lady? Why had her life had been cut so tragically short? Did she slip on the ice? Why wasn't she wearing a seat belt? Was she in a rush?* I thought back to my own car accident in the snow when I was sixteen. It had just begun to snow, but the makeup of the precipitation was mostly sleet. I was going to be late for school, I was going too fast for the weather situation and before I knew it my tiny car had locked up on a hill. I was picking up speed and could not steer, I was headed for the embankment, and a steep cliff. My car jumped the cliff, and the fall was broken by four large trees and then I blacked out. When I came to, I was in a hammock; my car holding me, and the trees holding the car, ten feet above the ground. I was very lucky but the Italian lady, sadly was not. Life is so fragile, and we take so much of it for granted, especially when we get behind the wheel of a car.

My accident at age sixteen got me thinking about pet peeves. When do they come to life and how? I would say my biggest pet peeve is feeling rushed. I have lived with anxiety for most of my life and it is made worse when I allow myself to feel rushed. My car accident was caused, at least in part, by the fact that I was rushing—well, at least in my mind, not in action. I was not speeding but my mind was distracted, I did not possess the focus required for driving in the snow, nor had I ever driven in it. That accident was not the only potentially life-threatening moment that resulted from rushing but more on that in a minute. Ironically, my husband says his biggest area for improvement is his patience and his biggest pet peeve, when people arrive late to a meeting or engagement he has scheduled. Our pet peeves might duke it out in a ring if we did not value healthy communication. Thankfully, I think his pet peeve has awakened my awareness of time and preparation over the years. Kevin is so good for me and to me! Anyway, I digress back to our discussion about pet peeves.

A second pet peeve I hold about myself is that I am a people pleaser and I do not like letting others down. I used to say yes to 95% of the things that were asked of me. Then at the end of the week I would find myself behind professionally, cranky with my family, unfocused, and just going through the motions of life. My kids would say my name multiple times while I pecked on my laptop, iPad, or iPhone. I was missing valuable time with my family and my kids felt invisible at times. I mentioned before that going through the motions in this gift called life is operating as a victim, but making intentional decisions is living as a fierce survivor. I used the word operating because being a victim does not feel like living, it feels robotic. We are not advised about how many days we have on this earth so living intentionally should be obvious but how many of us are allowing ordinary noise to distract us from the brisk quest of genuine meaning and purpose in our daily lives? In my case, the noise was the least of my problems, my avoidance of intentional living and tendency to be rushed in all things actually risked my life. It happened on an unassuming Tuesday at noon and scared me to death.

*   *   *   *

Going through the motions in this gift called life is operating as a victim, but making intentional decisions is living as a fierce survivor.

*   *   *   *

My husband and I were preparing for a general manager meeting, and twenty of our managers would arrive in a matter of minutes. I was printing agendas; he was setting up the power point. We had lunch delivered, steak kabobs and Greek salad. We only had five minutes to eat as the team would soon arrive. I do not remember all the details, but I swallowed a bite of steak that was too big and began to choke. I could not get the meat down, so I guzzled water. Then the water would not go down and I ejected it all over our conference table. Kevin tried to help me get the meat up but to no avail. We were both panicked and ran to the car. Thankfully, our office was five minutes from the hospital. Kevin drove like Jeff Gordon, sliding in and out of traffic like a pro and got us there safe and fast. I expelled more water in the emergency room lobby and the nurses brought me right back. I was given an IV and pumped full of muscle relaxers to try to get my throat to relax and the meaty morsel to release. I was able to breathe through my nose but having my throat closed off was very scary. I was tense preparing for the meeting and attempted to rush through lunch. This is a reoccurring theme in my life, feeling rushed and out of control of all aspects of my existence. It is also as if I have the word "overcommitted" permanently tattooed on my brain. Life is supposed to be fun and rewarding, not a blur of activities littering up your calendar. I needed to make a change but for some reason, that near-death experience did not catapult me into action.

It is funny, I mentioned earlier that sometimes God gives us clues when we are on the wrong course. I was given a few clues in the year that began with the almost choking incident. Several months later I was attending a business conference and managed to choke again on a piece of steak except I was surrounded by hundreds of people. I immediately ducked under the table trying to get the meat out of my throat and strongly considered becoming a vegetarian in that moment. Kevin helped me out of the event room, and I was able to get it out with a few hard smacks on the back. The difference is I was not racing around or stressed so how did it get stuck? When I returned home from the conference, I got a full blood work up. The doctor discovered that my thyroid hormone was elevated and scheduled me for an ultrasound and a series of scans. As soon as the technician took the first picture, the mystery was solved. I had a large nodule on the left side of my thyroid. The nodule and my regular appearance of out-of-control anxiety was a recipe for disaster. I began to understand this was a wake-up call, took the day off and scheduled a biopsy.

This would be my second guided needle biopsy on my neck; the first occurred when I was diagnosed with Non-Hodgkin's Lymphoma more than twenty years before. I was not looking forward to it, as you must remain very still, and the stinging pain of the needle makes staying still almost impossible. It took several weeks to get any answers, but eventually I was told the nodule was abnormal. I was absolutely stunned again and felt like I had just hit replay of the events from two decades before. How was this happening? Worst of all they could not get any further information until the nodule was surgically removed. My poor neck had been through enough, now another surgery, another huge scar but this time in the front of my neck. All I could think was I would soon look like Jack the Ripper's latest victim.

This would be the third very large scar on my neck and chest area, and of course there was the chance that I had cancer again. I pushed that possibility to the very back of my consciousness and made an appointment with a highly recommended surgeon. A few weeks later I was back in the hospital ready to get rid of the unwelcome attacker in my neck. The surgeon did an incredible job and the scar healed better than any of the others. Best of all, I did not have cancer. I breathed a deep sigh of relief and began to cross-examine the last year.

It did not take me long to realize that God had again sent me a very clear message. I was killing myself with the jam-packed schedule I was keeping. God knew the only way I would slow down was if I was made to do so. The recovery was a few weeks, and I could not talk much or work. I thought about how many times in a week I said yes. I thought about how many times I had to ask my kids to repeat themselves. I thought about feeling constantly rushed and unsuccessful with my to do lists. I was so tired and would sleep through my alarm clock and be late from the moment my feet hit the ground. I ate bad food on the run and had gained a ton of weight. I felt like a failure at every turn. Enough was enough and I finally pulled the trigger and learned to use a very important word, NO!

Saying no to people has always been a struggle for me but became less so when you feel your life depends on it. I had to prioritize my time more efficiently. Kevin and the children had always come first but I needed to be more present. Kevin and I were already having a date night once a week but now I put my phone down and am fully engaged with him. As a family we also try very hard to put our phones down at 7pm each night so we can enjoy quality, fully focused time with one another. When I am asked to attend events, I only attend one to two a month and before 5pm. When girlfriends invite me to dinners or wine night, I ask them to meet me for coffee or lunch. I keep my nights free so I can be with my husband and family as much as possible. I met my husband in my mid-thirties and soon my kids will all be in college, so it is time to enjoy every moment of that precious time with them.

I am very mindful about my calendar. I sit down on Sunday and map out the week. I aim to be productive; however, I have learned to stop over committing. Instead, I under promise and over deliver, which is usually a win for everyone. Beginning each day in my prayer retreat to get centered has made the most impact. I used to wake up at the last possible minute, rush through getting ready and dart out the door. Now I take my time, setting morning meetings no earlier than 9am and the absence of the morning sprint has made me feel more grounded than ever. I prep food each week and Kevin and I work as a team to make nutritious meals for our family. I exercise each morning to take care of my body and mind. Finally, I work very hard to be in the moment of wherever I am and whoever I am with.

I think about the Italian lady every now and then. Granted I do not know the story of her accident, but it was similar enough to mine that I take it as a sign. I do not allow myself to be rushed anymore because one decision can impact the consequences of your future. Our lives are a gift, and a fragile one at that. It always puzzles me when sitting in traffic how many people are eating, texting, and even doing their make-up while driving. Imagine how life changing it would be to do your make-up in your bathroom, eat at your table, and talk hands-free instead of texting. Life changing for many reasons, but most of important of all, you are not risking the lives of yourself and others. Block the time, it will be the best decision you ever made!

LIFE LESSON #8
Create a balance, set boundaries, and learn
to say no.

Have you ever been at an event talking to someone who seemed distracted, looking over your shoulder whenever someone else walked by? I used to be that person, the person who only half heard what you were saying, and I am embarrassed to admit that. I am the queen of setting unreasonable expectations for myself or a situation. My husband gave me a gift a few years ago and began pointing out how I ran myself ragged with little to show from it. I was so frustrated but thought the solution was to add more commitments to my calendar. Once I realized that I was making myself, and him, crazy I began to frame a new routine. I do not see friends often as I am a busy wife, mama, and business owner but when I do, I show up in mind, body, and spirit. What I realized was that I was thinking about what I had to do later in the day, and what I had not accomplished from the beginning of the day instead of engaging in the moment at hand. I had so many things on my calendar I was not able to invest in any of them. Once I eliminated the daily commitments by more than half, I was able to actually enjoy the engagements that had made the cut. I was also able to take care of myself with regard to nutrition, exercise, and sleep. I have been a part of the "No Club" for over a year now and I finally feel like I have control over my own life and my relationships have never been better! How is your calendar looking these days, my friend? How do you feel at the end of the week, satisfied or drained? What is one step you could take today to begin evaluating how you are spending your precious time?

CHAPTER 9
BECOMING "IZZY"

Did you always know what you wanted to be when you grew up? Or did you have a long list that started with traditional choices like doctor, lawyer, and teacher? Did you make the list based on your own interests, or what your parents suggested? What was the list based on, income, quality of life, prestige? How did you decide the criteria for that list? As I mentioned before, I have a lot of children, many of whom fall into the teenager category, so we are beginning these career conversations. It can be very stressful to try to figure out what you are going to choose to do for your career at age 18, or even earlier. The good news is you can always change your mind. I ran across a quote recently,

"Passion is the difference between having a
job or having a career." ~ Unknown

My favorite definition for passion can be found in the Urban Dictionary, I am including it for you below.

Definition: Passion
Urban Dictionary

"Passion is when you put more energy into something than is required to do it. It is more than just enthusiasm or excitement, passion is ambition that has materialized into action to put as much heart, mind, body, and soul into something as is possible."

Wow, that definition just took my breath away! But how do we find what we are passionate about? Most of us do not continue into a career from our first job. That does not mean; however, that we cannot gain valuable information about what type of work environment we prefer, which I believe to be one piece of the passion puzzle. When I was 15, I had my first job in customer service at a local dry cleaner. I really enjoyed the face-to-face interaction with people and looked forward to coming to work. I also loved my co-workers who eventually became friends. Several years later I had a job in the back of a news studio tracking weather and storms for a meteorologist in New Orleans. I was alone in a room with a computer, I hated feeling banished in a closet sized office and I only stayed in the job for a few months. I made twice the amount of money at the news channel than I did at the dry cleaner. These two experiences told me I prefer to work in a situation where I can interact with people and am not isolated, regardless of the pay. Most of us do not have the same career our entire working life. Discovering the various parts of what makes you passionate and how it can translate across industries is a great use of time and energy. I have lived through a divorce, moving with two small children to another state with no plan for work. As I write this many people are out of work because of the Covid-19 pandemic. The reality of life is we will likely have to reinvent ourselves to pay the bills. You may be surprised what you truly enjoy doing after some good soul searching.

As I mentioned before, I left my first husband without a plan for work. I had been teaching music to children four nights a week and singing in the ensemble with Opera Carolina. I was moving home to my small town and there were no openings to teach or sing. I also needed something during the day as I was a single parent. Taking the job at the law firm was going out on an extremely long, fragile limb. I did not have experience with legal documents, or intellectual property expertise, or most anything else in a law office setting. Then I took a moment and realized I had not been hired as a lawyer or a paralegal. I was hired to market the firm and bring in new clients. I loved interacting with people, so I chose to focus on that passion which made me excited to go to work each day. I also had a great deal of marketing experience from the Summer Opera Theatre Company in D.C. which gave me confidence. The other details of the job I learned in time. If you have at least one of your passion pieces represented, I believe you can be productive and fulfilled at least short term, even if the job is not in your dream industry.

One thing I learned during my transition: just because you are good at something does not mean you have to choose it as a career. I cannot tell you how many times in the last ten years I have been asked if I am still singing and if I plan to get back into it professionally. The answer is, no! It is really very interesting, I started singing in my early teens. God blessed me with that talent, and I am very grateful. I spent the first fifteen years of my career singing professionally. I know you are probably thinking, why in the world would you not be a performer if you have the talent and ability to do so? Let me tell you why. I loved singing to my kids as babies, sitting in their nurseries rocking them while singing songs off Celine Dion's album *Miracle* and *Disney's Princess Favorites*. I looked forward to the quality time with them and my voice seemed to soothe them. But when I would prepare a role for an opera or oratorio gig, I found myself procrastinating. Hesitating or stalling on a project does not equal passion.

Furthermore, I am an introvert so the idea of singing in front of thousands of people kept me up many nights with a blender of thoughts I could not turn off. What if I wake up with a sore throat? What if I forget the lyrics? What if I crack the high note? I was in a constant frenzy, feeling submerged and powerless in a pool of trepidation. If you can believe it, I actually enjoy speaking for large groups of people today. Perhaps this is because I have more control with my speaking voice than I did with my singing voice back in the day. Or perhaps a divine directive guided me through my own struggles to a place where I could understand and share them, potentially changing lives. Being able to change lives and help others all over the world should be everyone's passion in my humble opinion.

Also, when you are an opera singer it is suggested that you have a very specific diet with no dairy, caffeine, or wine as all these indulgences affect the voice. No ice cream or coffee, what?!?! Why would anyone choose to be that miserable? I kept thinking all these sacrifices would be a no brainer if this were what I loved more than anything else and if it was truly my #1 passion. Let us not forget that I was also able to have two perfect babies against all odds which was reason enough not to travel for work. Being a stay-at-home Mom for the first five years of their lives was the best decision I ever made. Watching them discover their own likes and dislikes. Witnessing the beginnings of talking and walking. Singing to them as they drifted off to sleep. There is nothing in this world that could have pulled me away from those precious babies, they will always be my greatest gift from God. Teaching and singing at night at that time made the most sense as it afforded me the most quality time with my children while they were awake.

Okay Mamas, do you remember when you had your first baby and your clothes were always painted with stains of spit up, your hair stringy with split ends on split ends on split ends, and dark circles under your eyes that even the best, most expensive foundation would not cover up? Now think about the day you were able to steal away a morning and go to Starbucks for a grande chai tea latte and banana bread followed by a quick trip to Marshall's to buy a new dress for an upcoming event all by yourself. The spectacular finale of that delightful solo outing was an hour visit with your "therapist" also known as your hair stylist while your husband takes care of the baby. How did that make you feel? Did you feel like a new woman? Was your day made? I think we will all agree that getting a fresh haircut and a new piece of clothing, after no self-love for months is magical. What if we could pick a career that allowed us to be the maker of other people's days every single day of our lives? What if we picked a career that allowed us to be the smile maker, the laugh doctor, or the anthropologist of happy? I learned in my research that there is a name for being a day maker.

Definition: Day Maker
Urban Dictionary
"A super cool person/event that makes somebody's whole entire day sometimes referred to as an Izzy."

When I married Kevin, he invited me to help him with local marketing in his Domino's franchise. Shortly thereafter Kevin asked me to run the business with him as a co-owner. I was very honored and accepted, we have worked together for the last seven years, and it has been wonderfully fulfilling. I am excited to share with you that in that time I have also identified the remaining pieces of my passion puzzle and have become a day maker myself. I became the point person for all donation requests for the business, and there were a lot. Our focus for giving remains children and families in need so I was able to filter through the requests relatively quickly. The requests usually included a story behind the ask and how the money or donation of food would assist the organization. Being able to give back to organizations in need and see them prosper was so cool and I felt like an Izzy! I also really loved the idea that our business delivered comfort in a box, as many people choose pizza on their worst days. The privilege of brightening the day of someone who just lost their job, is enduring a breakup, or is nursing sick kids at home with pizza is such a gift to my life. Knowing the impact our business has on people in all stages of life, and various situations is thrilling and completely satisfying.

Another role I took on was hiring management team members. I created a detailed script that told me everything I needed to know about a candidate from their core values to their work experience in thirty questions and sixty minutes. The interview conversations were fascinating! I loved hearing about life lessons that contributed to who the person had become. It was entertaining, and sometimes terrifying, to hear the stories of how the job seeker handled a difficult conflict in the workplace. My favorite part has always been "selling" our franchise to the prospective team member. I share with them our core values, our anti-gossiping campaign and kindness initiative, our team outings and family fun days, our income and career potential, and our charitable giving partnerships. I was so proud to paint the picture of how fulfilling and meaningful a career as a pizza leader could be! Many of our managers have come from a modest or often unhappy upbringing. Most did not attend college but have been able to grow with us and become general managers and even supervisors without higher education. Who knew that I could make an impact in the lives of people in need and individuals searching for a rewarding career with tremendous opportunities to advance? The puzzle was coming together, and I had never been happier.

My husband celebrated thirty years with the Domino's brand a couple years ago. I had a beautiful fire shaped glass award made for him with the following quote,

"Be fearless in the pursuit of what sets your
soul on fire." ~ Jennifer Lee

That is passion. Feeling your soul ignite from the excitement of a new project, the impact you are having in the world, or a big win achieved in the face of uncertainty. Passion means you do not want to turn it off; you are happy to keep working past five p.m. or taking a call from a colleague or customer on a Sunday. You eat, sleep, and breathe this career, because it is the one you were destined to choose.

Ally & Kevin, Domino's Headquarters, 2019

Ally & Kevin, Gold Franny Awards, 2018

I mentioned the passion puzzle earlier regarding choosing your career and I believe there are five essential pieces that make up that magical circle. It is very easy to remember because my passion puzzle is made up of five parts that begin with p!

The #fiercetigerlady Passion Puzzle

Positivity.
You look forward to going to work and are happy while you are there.

Preferred work environment.
I touched on this earlier. Basically, do you prefer to work alone or around other people? Additionally, do you enjoy a fast paced or more relaxed work environment?

Purpose.
You feel as though there is a deeper meaning or directive at play and that keeps you inspired at work.

Potential to grow.
You are motivated by the ability to grow personally or professionally because of the experience. Perhaps you are also learning a new skill set.

Personality type
You have taken either (or both) the Enneagram or Myers-Brigg's personality tests and that information has helped you to be better connected to your ultimate career match.

Let us discuss personality types! Allow me to encourage you to invest in the endeavor of understanding yourself better by taking the Enneagram and/or Myers-Brigg's tests if you have not already. I took the Myers-Brigg's test many years ago as part of the curriculum in a year-long leadership course. I took the Enneagram test two years ago while working closely with a business coach. To take the Enneagram test go to tests.enneagraminstitute.com and purchase the RHETI test for $12. This is the affordable option. If you would like to invest $175 to take Myers-Brigg's it is worth every penny as I have continued to use the information received for over a decade. The Enneagram explores nine personality types while Myers-Briggs navigates sixteen.

The Enneagram test actually labeled me equal parts of two personality types which I thought was interesting. I am 50/50 The Helper (#2) and The Peacemaker (#9.) The interesting thing about this personality test is that it digs into how periods of stress and periods of growth affect how you show up for other people. It is a very interesting resource if you are trying to understand yourself better.

The Myers-Brigg's personality test labeled me as an INFJ personality or "Advocate." An "Advocate" (INFJ) is someone with introverted, intuitive, feeling, and judging personality traits. I was shocked to see that INFJ is the rarest type and when I read the pages and pages of insight, I was better equipped to design a life that allows me to show up as my best possible self. There is a ton of useful information behind the four letters that make up the unique sixteen personality types at Myers-Briggs. To find out more about the test, the sixteen personality types or to actually take the test go to www.MBTIonline.com.

These two personality tests have taught me a lot about myself and allowed me to complete my passion puzzle. The reoccurring themes in the pages of information provided by the Enneagram and Myers-Brigg's are fascinating. I learned that my driving purpose in life is to help others. I also figured out that even though I am an introvert, I enjoy speaking to groups about subjects I am passionate about, for instance survival and triumph after trauma. Purpose and passion are a winning combination because purpose is just passion with its work-boots on. I am most alive when I work with a hurting individual to craft a solution that changes their present situation and, in turn, their future. I also realized that my deeply depressed, anxiety charged traumaniacal season was likely caused by neglecting my own self-care for two decades. My self-care needs are firmly rooted in being outdoors, surrounded by nature. Realizing this was the first step in recovery because how can we effectively care for others if we are not healthy in our own bodies and minds?

* * * *

Purpose is just passion with its work-boots on.

* * * *

In my research I also found three female leaders that share my personality type. I am including their names, personality types and impactful quotes below. I think when we can find connection with strong leaders who understand our strengths and struggles from the inception of our personality infrastructure we can grow in our own leadership ability at a deeply profound level. We should be having more conversations about personality types and finding companionship (and mentorship) with someone who is kin to your personality is a great opportunity for understanding and improvement. My INFJ personality type is actually the rarest personality type, accounting for somewhere around 3% of the population who has taken Myers-Brigg's. I was thrilled to see that I share this personality type with the "Queen of All Media," Oprah Winfrey! I doubt she will be taking me on as a mentoree anytime soon; however, knowing that we share the same personality qualities makes me want to dig into her published wisdom that much more! I believe when we understand what makes our personality tick, we are better equipped to make important decisions and lead impactful lives. My personality traits also helped me to confidently nail down my professional passions and resulted in my finding my perfect match in my career—first as a core values leader and business owner and now as a passionate writer who wants to help others with my story.

With the good, there is usually some measure of bad. The negative part of being an INFJ is that we are hard critics on ourselves, hence the "judging" characteristic represented by the "J." It is difficult to be patient with the steady progression of projects and goals, and the delayed success can cause mental or emotional collapses (or both.) The extreme result is a blustery temper that flares like a raging wildfire fueled by disappointment and unrealistic expectations. My balance of daily self-care (see Chapter 1) and setting healthy expectations have kept my fiery temper at bay, but it is a threat I must actively control with mindfulness when stress is high.

All personality types exist on a spectrum of good and bad. Some people thrive with the power that comes from their unique character and some use it for evil. Oprah is at *heaven status* in my opinion but there are two INFJs that reside at hell status...Adolf Hitler and Osama Bin Laden. Yep, you read that right. I cannot imagine a more extreme range of good and bad, can you? I was shocked when I found out that I shared a personality type with two notorious centaurs; however, it also encourages me to always be grateful for the ability to lead others for the greater good. I realize I used the fire metaphor as a reference for both good and bad in this chapter. Wildfires are characteristically out of control and dangerous while a single flame symbolizes passion and rebirth. Just like the personality, fire exists on a spectrum that spans creative motivation at the top, and our deadly demise at the bottom. The personality can be a tool or a weapon and understanding how it is nurturing you at your best and destroying opportunity at its worst is a good use of time when considering your future.

Ok enough of the heavy, now let me share my three personality heroes with you! My personality heroes are confident, kind, smart, generous humanitarians. Who are your personality heroes and how are they inspiring you to understand yourself better and find your ultimate passion?

My Personality Heroes

Oprah Winfrey (INFJ)
"Know what sparks the light in you. Then
use that light to illuminate the world."

Audrey Hepburn (#9)
"For beautiful eyes, look for the good in
others; for beautiful lips, speak only words
of kindness; and for poise, walk with the
knowledge that you are never alone."

Eleanor Roosevelt (#2)
"No one can make you feel inferior without your consent."

LIFE LESSON #9
When considering your future,
always choose passion over pennies!

If you had told me at age eighteen that I would eventually be a business owner in a pizza franchise, I would have said you were nuts. This career is about the farthest thing from an opera singer, but you know what, I love it a million times more than I ever loved singing professionally. God always has a plan, and it can be far from the plan you originally had in mind. Be open to what is revealed, allowing yourself time to evaluate the option that is presented. Listen to your mind, body, and soul—they will give you cues. I should have known that sleepless nights and constant worry were not a recipe for success or happiness, but I continued to do it because I was making money.

Money does not mean much when you are so mentally exhausted from the effort it takes to walk up on the stage, feeling like an impostor. As you can imagine, the opera world is also notorious for insincerity and sabotage. As a rookie college student, I beat out a list of other singers for a highly coveted role. You would have thought I had burned down their house, the hostile vibes were absurd, and I remember thinking that I was surrounded by children. I could not function long term in that negativity. I have always prided myself on being positive and choose to surround myself with positive people. Afterall, we are the average of the five people we spend the most time with. Who are you spending your time with? Do your friends bring out the best in you? Do your co-workers cheer you on and collaborate professionally? Do you have reciprocal conversations with the people in your life, or is it all one sided? I believe the secret formula for a happy life is comprised of three essential elements: positivity, passion, and purpose! Are you living these three elements in your daily life or does your formula need some attention?

*　*　*　*

I believe the secret formula for a happy life is comprised of three essential elements: positivity, passion, and purpose!

* * * *

Take some time to make a list of all the jobs you have held and the pros and cons in each role. Highlight all the pros, also known as passions, and see if there is a pattern. My list included: social work environment, day maker opportunities, a schedule that allows me to be with my children as much as possible (I can do some work from home), creative writing time and divine purpose occasions to help others. Keep a mood journal and make sure you are excited to go to work each day, fueled with positivity! What would growth look like in your perfect position? Is it related to being promoted up the corporate ladder or developing a new skill set on a more personal level? Finally, define and evaluate the level of purpose you are expressing in your daily life. Is the purpose being cultivated by your passion? Also remember that you can develop new passions at any time in your life, there are no rules about this. For example, I have always had a passion for people but my newer passion for writing coupled with people set off an electric current that charged my purpose to write this book! I hope these suggestions shed light on questions you are asking yourself about your career choices and decisions, my friend. It is never too late to make a change for your ultimate happiness and career gratification. Have fun with your research and I hope you find the profession that sets your soul on fire!

CHAPTER 10
THE QUARANTINE

<u>Captain's log, day 182.</u>
Cabin fever is rampant like large waves
during a sea storm, the crew has gone into
hiding and hope has left the ship...

In the intro of this book, I shared a precious encounter with
a baby tiger. Now allow me to share a not so precious moment with an adult tiger. I was back on *the Strip*; it was October in Vegas. A warm dessert breeze caused the litter from
last night's party to spin and shift in the street, and tourists
were wearing jackets. My husband was pulled into a meeting, so I decided to take a quick walk down to the Mirage.
I had an hour to kill and was giddy with excitement to visit
with the tigers. The habitat is a serpentine shape that winds
around approximately ten enclosures and includes tigers, lions, jaguars, panthers, cougars, and leopards.

I bought my ticket and began my walk in the Secret Garden. Immediately, I observed a massive male lion sleeping
peacefully on a large tree. His majestic blonde fur framed his
elegant face, and his oversized paws were crossed as if to say,

"Do not disturb." The jaguar and leopard were also asleep. It was hard to function in that dry dessert heat as a human; imagine what it's like with all that fur? Looking ahead I saw a small crowd was beginning to assemble near the tigers. Suddenly I was overcome with the site of a majestic orange and black tiger pacing in his habitat. As I got closer, I could see he was panting feverishly and was clearly in a panic. A female tiger was behind me in a separate enclosure and was less agitated. One of the animal caregivers explained to the group of us that the female tiger was in heat and the male tiger did not like all of us between him and "his woman."

Protective Tiger, Mirage Resort, Vegas, 2019

I giggled and blushed slightly as I finally felt like I had found the man who would love and protect me as this concerned tiger attempted to safeguard his tiger woman. Distracted in the moment of my own wedded bliss, I was brought back to reality when the male tiger uttered a terrifying roar. Even more alarming, the roar was directed at me and the two kids standing nearby. Without warning, the tiger lifted his leg and released his bladder all over me and the kids as we stared, frozen and dumbfounded. Had that *really* happened, had I just been pissed on by a huge, angry four-hundred-pound tiger? Yep, that happened. That really happened, and it was awful! I bring it up because I think it is fair to say that all of us have felt "pissed on" one, two, ten times in 2020, am I right? So how do we survive? How do we get up, wash off the stinky pee and remain positive despite the adversity that seems to reoccur this year for so many of us? How do we get out of the "Murphy's Law" mentality that appears to be around every corner of this cursed year?

Today marks day 182 of the COVID19 virus quarantine. Day 182 of teenagers complaining of the struggles of mobile learning, not seeing their friends, and being bored. Day 182 of feeling like a failure because I am not equipped to tutor high school level math and science. Day 182 of attempting to work from home with constant distraction from my neighbor's home improvement projects which sound like a "Fixer Upper" demo day followed by the timely onset of barking dogs, lawn mowers, or turbulent rainstorms. Day 182 of sky-high anxiety every time someone in our home coughs or sneezes. Day 182 of cooking, cleaning, and laundry as the task of summoning the teenagers for help takes more energy than I have left. Day 182 of conference calls on mute and 30% power because I cannot find a quiet spot in my house and my charger has gone missing again. Day 182 of starting my diet again for the hundredth time as chocolate chip cookies and Goldfish seem like a good alternative to therapy, which is not available anyway. Day 182 of date nights consisting of a masked-up mad dash through Target to get the last pack of toilet paper and last bottle of 409 spray cleaner superseded by a romantic trip though the Chick fil 'A drive thru. Finally, Day 182 also brought a phone call that triggered my traumas from over twenty years ago. Traumas that I never addressed. Traumas that would continue to stop me in my tracks if I did not deal with them once and for all. On Day 182 I decided enough is enough and I raised my white flag, admitted defeat of attempting to strong arm it through my health crisis related stress, and surrendered to God.

I absolutely love to travel and have been able to visit some truly breathtaking places. As I mentioned before, I spent a month in Italy in college and recall a picturesque day spent on the rugged cliffs on the Island of Capri. Capri is known for the Blue Grotto, a stunning underwater cave. I found myself transfixed as I watched the sun light up the sea's cavern, reflecting a gorgeous metallic tapestry that resembled the scales of a mermaid's tail. The mirrored flickering of green, blue, and gold color combinations would go unnoticed on a cloudy day, created a gallery of stunning art beneath the waves. The sun reflected off my sunglasses and warmed my chilled skin and I almost forgot it was the middle of winter. It was such a quiet moment, despite the chaos of my rebellious classmates diving off the cliff with muffled screams as they descended into ice cold water. To find the quiet in that moment seemed a miracle, yet I found it.

Ally, Island of Capri, Italy, 1996

I think most of us would agree it is difficult if not impossible to focus on anything meaningful in the crazy dumpster fire of 2020. Can I get an AMEN? God tells us in in Psalm 46:10, "Be still, and know that I am God." So, what does that mean? To me it says, stop fighting and listen for his word. Has this year been a fight? A battle every single day to get up and do the bare minimum? How are you showing up for your family? Are you wearing the same pjs and makeup for the last 3 days and wondering why your kids look worried? Are you being nudged by God to do something with this gift of time that we almost never receive?

In my case that nudge did not feel like a gift. The call I received on Day 182 was from my doctor. She called to notify me that the pre-cancerous cells that had invaded my reproductive area two years before had returned. The same pre-cancerous cells that had been cut or burned out of my body three times before in five years. There was only one more option on the table, a hysterectomy. The call ended and suddenly it was 1995 and 1997 and 2000 and 2002 and 2003 and 2019 again. The curse of affliction had found me again and I could not fathom how I would endure another fight for my health. I started down the rabbit hole of negativity, my mind replaying all the nightmares on a loop. The complicated labyrinth always brings me back to the same idea that somehow, I had invited all of this misery into my life. I had to break the cycle once and for all.

Being stuck in your home for months on end is also a great time to take on a project! The project I chose was breaking that reoccurring cycle and unpacking the baggage of my past traumas and working toward peace through forgiveness. This is a big project, huge in fact. How was I going to forgive Stan and Ethan for sexually abusing and raping me?? In Chapter 3 and 5 I was able to use my voice and my pen to release the shame I was feeling about both predatory encounters; however, the idea of forgiving Stan or Ethan seemed impossible, yet God seemed to be nudging me that way. I began by googling "bible verses about forgiveness" and recited the first five that popped up. Unfortunately, I felt no movement in my stubborn heart toward the idea of forgiveness. I needed help and thankfully God provided just the help I needed. One of my heroes visited me during my quest to connect with the idea of forgiveness.. Janelle is an amazing woman of God, trauma survivor, writer, leader, and friend. She is also the founder of "Emerging Life Coaching" and has been my business and life coach for the last two years. Our discussions exist in various categories; building strength in my business by utilizing energy leadership, harnessing my personality attributes as a "Peacemaker" and "Helper," and using said attributes to look for opportunities to explore passions that are yet defined, and on our most recent visit, we discussed my traumas. Some of these traumas I had never even told my husband until recently. I took a deep breath and recounted the horrific five years of chronic trauma I had endured and without warning, I began to cry. It was surprising to me that I was able to cry about any of it because when you choke down trauma for decades, typically you, or at least I, disconnect from the physical process of grief.

I realized something profound in that moment. I needed to do more than write it all down. I needed to bravely speak out loud about the traumas I had endured, I needed to wear the tears proudly and begin the process of forgiveness in its entirety. Comprehensive forgiveness means I had to forgive myself first and then I had to forgive those who hurt me which seemed absurd. Janelle's advice to me was to untie myself from each trauma, one by one, and give God permission to do the work of forgiveness on my heart and soul. Today I am starting that journey with forgiving myself. I have been very hard on myself over the years and my inner dialogue was not one of love. That day I began the process of flipping the script and I will no longer say that my body is cursed. I will forgive myself for saying such a harsh thing and believe that abundant health is still attainable! I will forgive myself for the blame and shame I carried for years after I was abused by two predators, I am not hauling that heavy burden one day longer. Finally, I am forgiving myself for the many times in my life I have hurt another person with my words or actions. Today is a new day and all our regrets can be transformed into lessons that allow us to make amends and live freely through the process of forgiveness.

A couple of days after Janelle's visit, I met Krisha for drinks at our local wine bar. The wine bar, appropriately named "Blacksburg Wine Lab" has been a gift to our small town since January 2018. The charming locale, owned by two brilliant Virginia Tech professors, is the perfect place for date night or Sunday brunch as the food is equally delicious. The dimly lit lounge, fashions rustic local wood walls that house international wines from all over the world, regional art and a gorgeous grape inspired chandelier that creates an unmatched ambiance. That happy hour with Krisha landed on my calendar just over ten years from the night of my 34th Birthday party Krisha had planned for me. Ten years had passed and as I waited for Krisha, at her favorite table, I felt so thankful for this special woman who had changed my life a decade ago. The woman who used her expert connecting skills to help me find a job, and soon after, the love of my life. I decided tonight was the night I would put on the training wheels and put this book idea into motion. I would also continue to unhitch myself from blame in my past sexual abuse traumas by the steady progression of speaking about them out loud with someone I trust.

I had successfully shared my sexual abuse traumas with my husband, Janelle, and that night I planned to share them with Krisha. She had been my friend from age four and it seemed like a good way to gauge my level of comfortability sharing deeply personal events from my past. Our Blacksburg High School classmate, and tonight's waiter John began pouring the Jansz Rosé from Tasmania and returned to his post at the bar. It is such a gift to be able to reconnect with high school friends decades later and John was one of my favorites. He was an expert at conversation in a variety of obscure topics and you would never meet a better cocktail creator and wine connoisseur. I took a copious sip, a deep breath, and ripped off the band aid. I disclosed my traumas to Krisha, the torturous story of Stan, and then Ethan. I used the same slang, "the back door," when explaining the details of Ethan's attack as those words seemed much more lady like in comparison to "anal rape." Krisha's eyes brimmed with tears and her compassion was palpable. She took my hand in hers, her empathy and kindness caused my fear to dissipate, and I had my sign. This story, my story, was something other women needed to hear. My story could save someone from a brutal rape or worse. I felt a surge of energy and confidence, it was time to share my traumas and the life lessons I took from them with the world.

We sat in silence for a few moments and for the first time ever in my life, I was not worried about being judged and finally felt free. Krisha took a few extra minutes to process all the information I shared and then quietly whispered, "I am so sorry, and how awful that he broke in through your back door to attack you." I paused for a couple of seconds confused and finally realized she did not understand my creative attempt at slang. I mean it is not as if there is a rule book about how to tell someone you have been raped in the worst imaginable way. Once I figured out what had happened, I broke out into an absolute roar of laughter. Not just a polite chuckle, a full out erupting belly laugh that left me sore the next day. I think Krisha probably thought I was a little bit nuts at that juncture but that full out, unapologetic guffaw was just what the doctor ordered. I should have probably used the word sodomize when explaining the rape but had not quite mustered up the courage to use that term. No matter, I felt so free and was able to forgive myself for the years of shame I had carried for the sexual abuse I endured.

I had unpacked the incestuous sexual abuse and disgraceful ass-rape in a matter of months. I was still a work in progress with regards to forgiving Stan and Ethan but the hot scorching wildfire of hate I felt for both of them was now more of a casual flickering flame on my Bath and Body Works fresh balsam candle. I could still see and smell the once smoldering forest, now warm and subtly fragrant, a reminder of what I endured but no dangerous structure-destroying flames remained. The transfer of identity in the fire from pure anger to the single flame of hope through the process of forgiveness was life changing. I am still a work in progress, but I see myself growing through the steady progression of exoneration from my past. The miraculous thing I have come to realize about beginning the process of forgiving those who attempted to destroy me is that I am taking my power back by forgiving them. Holding on to grudges and hate for decades only makes you feel worse. By actively forgiving you are allowing your best self to shine through.

Forgiveness means you no longer hide behind a veil of secrets and shame. You stand proud, face to the sky showing the world the authentic, beautiful person God has seen all along. Try standing proud with a Wonder Woman pose and see how energized you become as you have truly earned that title after completing the strenuous task of forgiving your enemies! I am entering the final mile of forgiving my earthly enemies but now it is time to tackle the reoccurring health battles and the mind games I have played repeatedly with myself since I was twenty years old. I have allowed the health battle game card to be facilitated by the Devil and that ends today. His rules are unfair and affect the way I see myself and my ability to fight. I am a #fiercetigerlady, and my roar is loud enough to muffle the lies the enemy tries to implant in my vulnerable moments. Permit me to share the most recent health battle and what I learned from it.

On October 22, 2020 I had my tenth surgery and invited five more scars to accompany the three I already had. My scars are located on my neck, chest and abdomen and I have been slightly obsessed with them. The one on my chest is an ugly keloid that lost its shape, pulled down by the weight of my breasts. I have had many people ask me about that scar over the years; massage therapists, doctors, friends, and strangers and frankly, it used to tick me off. First, it is none of their business and second, the inquiry always came right at the point I had forgotten I even had that scar and inevitably all those dreadful memories came running back into my mind. Recently I ran across an important quote,

"A scar simply means you were stronger than whatever tried to hurt you." Unknown

Well look at that, a positive reference to my superficial defect. I realized I had to get stronger, in body and mind and see the scars for what they really represent. My eight scars are reminders of my brave fight with cancer and most recently, the newest scars symbolize that I was able to head cancer off at the pass this time. Who cares about a scar when it means you do not have cancer this time! Holy Cow, Ally…

wake up and realize how very lucky you are to just have a scar and not a scar and more chemo or a scar followed by radiation…or death.

The other mind game that I allowed to rule me is that my immune system is permanently damaged. Yes, there is some truth to that. Non-Hodgkin's Lymphoma did a number on my immune system, but I have learned to protect myself as much as humanly possible as far as air-born threats are concerned. Both sets of abnormal cells that invaded my thyroid and my reproductive area were likely more fortuitous in their attack because of my somewhat depressed immune system but as I said in Chapter 2, we have a choice about our mindset. I believe it is possible to manifest the worst possible outcome from our afflictions if our mind is not strong and positive. I had to take back my power by addressing the details of the health battles that were in my control and thankfully, there were a handful of things that were under my jurisdiction. What areas of your current adversity are within your control? What would it feel like to focus on only those things instead of worrying about the things that only God has control of? I can tell you! It feels like freedom. Not only freedom, but it also feels like you are slapping Satan in his big ugly face by continuing to have a smile on yours. Do not allow that evil to take you down. Take your power back!

I was starting to maneuver the muck of years of mind games. That journey also required me to take a long, honest look at how I was caring for my body. The answer, I had not been caring for it at all. As I mentioned before, in July 2019 half of my thyroid was removed after a large abnormal nodule appeared. Thankfully, I dodged the bullet on this one too, as the abnormal cells turned out to be benign. That is good news; however, thyroid issues are often caused by unbalanced hormones. I had been asking for this for years with my reckless lifestyle of no exercise, too much wine, processed foods before vegetables and my daily sugar fix. My body was giving me signals but it has taken me almost two additional years to get off the couch and do something about it. I had to take my own advice (from Chapter One) and get into a routine, a routine to get healthy and strong! So…what did I do? Two months after my hysterectomy I sat down with my husband and we decided that 2021 is our year, our year to get our health in line. For the last several years we have had a lot of stress in many areas of our life, and we coped with it by using food and alcohol. For us to progress toward abundant health we had to agree to hold each other accountable, therefore we decided to craft a plan together. Our plan is as follows; in case you are looking for inspiration.

Exercise: We stay active and exercise every day. We mix it up, so we do not get bored. Here are some of the activities we choose to do to take care of our bodies. The key for us was doing it together so we could act as each other's accountability partner. Additionally, doing a lot of different activities engages different muscles and confuses the body, allowing for steady change if you are looking to lose weight.

Play basketball with the kids.

Play tennis with each other.

Daily walks after dinner.

Long hikes or walks on the weekends (10 miles).

HIIT Peleton bike rides several times a week or if the weather is bad.

Pilates two times a week to keep our core muscles strong.

Weightlifting two times a week to keep all the other muscles strong.

Nutrition: We use the 16:8 model of intermittent fasting and eat in a window of ten a.m. to six p.m. We eat clean, unprocessed foods with a focus on lean proteins, a variety of vegetables and whole grains. We use the "My Fitness Pal" app to keep track of our food intake and weight loss. We also drink one hundred ounces of water a day. The only other thing we drink is one clean coffee or hot tea, meaning no artificial sweeteners or creamers packed with chemicals. Once we reach our goal weights, we will likely add two glasses of wine a week on our date night. You must enjoy your life; but everything in moderation, my friend.

I can report that since we began this new routine, I have never felt better. I have a crazy amount of energy and sleep through the night, a full eight hours! The commitment to health has also realigned my focus for my family and work. I feel more present for my kids and am checking more items off my list than I ever did. I take the time to celebrate wins like losing inches, not just pounds. I had not celebrated anything for myself in a long time and choosing to focus on my present positives has left very little time to dwell on the past. I figured out quickly that the best way to untie myself from the trauma of cancer and other health adversities was to get this body strong and not continue to fill it with crap. The hardest realization that came from the distraction of adversity was the fact that I used alcohol and emotional eating to numb the painful clamoring of my past traumas and current stress. The thing many people do not realize is that alcohol worsens anxiety and for me, already having anxiety, I was a mess. It takes a lot of courage to wake up one day and boldly declare, I am taking my power back and finally making the change. I am not going to lie, I have attempted the health goal many times but this time, I promise you I will succeed. This time, the love of my life is on board and our beautiful future is at stake. I cannot wait to tell you all about this journey and all the things we learned along the way. For now, please give yourself grace for whatever is holding you back. Forgive yourself for the heavy baggage you are carrying that caused you to say something hurtful you did not mean. Exonerate yourself from the hate you have felt for yourself and others and give it over to God. Wipe the slate clean and be strong enough to set some goals that allow you to shine as the amazing person you are.

A couple of paragraphs ago I was talking to you about taking our control back during affliction by focusing on the details that we do have control over. I am going to share these with you because I truly feel like they made the difference with my recent surgery.

I prayed every single day, asking God to heal my body.

I recited positive affirmations, determined to achieve abundant health once the current battle is won. I am on that journey now! Flipping the script on the negative inner dialogue is tough but if you say positive phrases over and over, the dialogue slowly becomes reprogrammed.

I redirected my mind when it attempted to take a trip to *negative town* by going on a walk or calling my husband.

I hired the best possible medical team. I asked lots of questions.

I never miss a doctor's appointment and stay on top of my health and symptoms.

I make better nutrition choices; my diet is now whole food based.

I stopped drinking for two months to detox any potential hazards.

I became an active person and burn a minimum of 2000 calories a day. The iPhone Fitness app helps me keep track of how active I am from day to day.

I put a big focus on my mental health and began talking through my fears and anxiety with a therapist.

I also stay on top of my anxiety medication, if it is not working, I talk with my doctor to tweak the dosage.

I make plans and even if the current week is impossibly hard, I have something to look forward to. (Krisha moved three hours away and in two weeks I am going to see her for lunch!)

Now it is your turn! Which aspects can you control in your affliction? Maybe start your list with forgiveness and allow that freedom to give you fresh eyes to see beyond your current storm. What is something you have been wanting to do and you keep making excuses about why you have not done it? Put it on your calendar so you have something to look forward to! You can do this; I believe in you!

LIFE LESSON #10
Take your control back and find
freedom in forgiveness.

Praise the Lord, 2020 has come to an end. I asked you earlier, how do we get through the "Murphy's Law" mentality that has haunted us this entire year? When it feels like every week there is a new nightmare in the news. When you are questioning the presence of humanity in the world. When you are so engrossed in the current crisis that you have allowed your routine to be stunted to a grinding halt four days this week. It is easy to get wrapped up in all the could have, should have, and would haves in life but you are truly wasting your time. What has happened is over and we can either allow it to ruin us or we can learn from the lesson. The lesson is not always fun, but we become stronger people because of it.

Believe me, I used to HATE to exercise but once I found a type of exercise that I liked, it absolutely clicked for me. We are not all marathon runners; however, there are countless ways to stay active. Start by taking a walk around the block with your dog or commit to one class a week at your gym. Making a pledge to achieve abundant health has allowed me a sharpened focus to tie up the loose ends with my past traumas and be "all in" regarding the forgiveness process. You might say a two for one, ha ha! It is no accident, as I asked God to repair those gaping wounds in my heart, but it took time and prayer to understand where to begin.

I believe the first step is evaluating your life and focusing on the areas that are within your control. What sections are keeping you in chains? Which relationships need your attention? What would freedom feel like and what are you willing to sacrifice to get there? Stop blaming yourself and living in the shame shadow of your past. Why are you stuck there? Is Satan holding you hostage? What is Satan saying to you? Is he whispering to you that you are a bad person and deserve to be where you are? Is he suggesting you play the victim because it takes less energy than taking your power back? Is he telling you that being negative is cooler than finding your authentic smile and positivity? CUT THE DEVIL OFF! You must delete the negativity and toxic inner dialogue from your reality. You can have a totally different life starting today, craft a healthy strategy for forgiveness and move forward! You have control over your thoughts so start today by forgiving yourself. I believe in you, gorgeous (handsome), now get to it!

CHAPTER 11
BETTE

Do you remember a few moments ago when I danced a jig and valiantly celebrated that 2020 was over? Then I went a step further, bolding proclaiming that 2021 was my year? Well…apparently the Devil heard me and cued up another fiery curve ball to knock the celebratory champagne right out of my glass is half full mentality. Buckle up, friend… this trauma was the hardest one of all.

Mother nature awoke in the wee hours of morning enraged and inflicted her arctic fury on the East Coast. Texas residents were stunted in the morning commute by a treacherous icy surface that caused a 133-car pile-up and left six people dead. In Virginia, the freezing rain covered branches and stems of sturdy and fragile trees. The Japanese maples looked like sculpted art but called out with muffled chimes, waiting for the sun to release the heavy burden. The pines and oaks stood with greater confidence, but the limbs soon dipped to expose a deceptive threat, as they canopied frail homes and old cars parked beneath them. The moon illuminated the dense fog that enveloped our small town and it felt like a shroud of prophesy. Seven hours before the storm began, an ambulance carried my mother-in-law, Bette, from our home. Her breast cancer had returned with a vengeance and the end of her precious life had been marked by days. The savage storm predicted the beginning of the end and all the future plans we had made with Bette were seized from our reality.

Almost ten years earlier...

I remember the day I met Bette as if it were yesterday. It was the spring of 2011; I had been dating Kevin for a couple of months. I changed my outfit three times before Kevin picked me up, hoping to make a good first impression. We met in the parking lot of a busy chain restaurant in Roanoke, Virginia and as the wind urged us through the front door, I knew I liked her immediately. Bette's laugh and handshake were warm, her smile, honest and her eyes, full of wisdom and experience. I loved the name, Bette; it represented elegance and tradition to me, and the Dutch/English origin, "God's promise" was very fitting as she was a devoted woman of God. Her name and persona seemed synonymous with many of the strong women I admired from my own family, Susan, Harriet, Margaret, Caroline, Dorothy, Josephine. Bette's middle name, Lee, is also my Daddy's middle name which was the first of many discoveries we had in common. Bette stood at five feet tall, with size five "Cinderella" feet, stunning white hair complemented her olive skin, and the thickness of her perfectly curled short hair was a gift all women wish they had. I have always admired how women of her generation took the time to put themselves together with perfect hair and make-up no matter their plans for the day. These classy ladies are always *picture ready* while many of us are sporting yoga pants, messy buns, and yesterday's make-up for a quick run to the grocery store. Bette's influence in the beauty department always inspired me to want to do more and try harder to be a refined classy lady like herself.

We took our seats in an expansive booth and began to explore the menu. Bette ordered the Monte Cristo sandwich and as I watched her enjoy the sweet and savory marriage of buttery bread, turkey, ham, melty cheese, powdered sugar, and raspberry jam it was clear to me she was a polished lady inside and out as not one drop of jam or speck of sugar met her proper pink jacket. My attempt to eat the same sandwich would have exposed a hot mess complete with stains on my carefully selected dress, no doubt about that. Bette and I both shared a love of desserts, and I admired her ability to indulge without guilt. Up until her illness, she had also gone to the gym every day. I had never met anyone who was as active as she was at seventy years young. She was the perfect role model of balance, savoring the pleasures of life while upholding her commitments and promises.

A stranger's observation of Bette's life would potentially reveal a quiet, unassuming existence but they would be wrong. In May of 2013 Bette became my mother-in-law and she allowed me to embark on an expedition, discovering all the dynamic ways she touched the lives of all who were blessed to know her. The title mother-in-law gets a bad rep. Have you seen "Monster in Law?" Jane Fonda's character certainly scared many a girl away from getting more serious with their man. Having a mother-in-law was a new experience for me at age thirty-six, as my first husband's mother had passed before we met. Bette had been around the same age as I was then when she lost her husband Dallas, Kevin's Daddy. Dallas fought Lymphoma bravely but lost his battle when Kevin was only eleven years old and his sister Melinda, sixteen. When Dallas passed Bette had been taking care of her family as a full-time stay-at-home Mom and lived five hours away from both hers and Dallas' parents. This is the moment in the retelling of her life story that Bette became my personal hero. A more delicate person would have given up, moved home, and admitted defeat but not Bette, she was determined to stay in Roanoke. Do not allow her petite frame to fool you, she was an absolute warrior!

Bette was the oldest of four daughters and had the best parts of her determined Daddy championing her forward after tragedy. She was an expert multi-tasker; she loved and consoled her devastated children, began an almost forty-year career with Blue Ridge Cancer Care, and was able to continue to own their family home all while cooking a homemade meal every single night. She was a busy lady but still managed to inoculate life's most important lessons to her children. The day of Bette's passing I read the following Bible verse and encouragement from Carolyn Larsen.

"If a man will not work,
he shall not eat." Thessalonians 3:10

Carolyn Larsen then goes on to say, "Teach your children the joy of hard work. Let them work side by side with you doing yard work and housework. Let your children experience the joy of a completed job. Instill good work ethics in your children."

It was no accident that God put these words before me, giving me the opportunity to share it with the world as one of Bette's greatest legacies. The work ethic she demonstrated as a single mother inspired her son to become a very successful entrepreneur, and motivated leader who continues to spark those around him into action. We honored Bette with a gold "Grammy" inspired award on Kevin's 30th Anniversary with the Domino's brand, stating that his phenomenal success was a product of her impressive fortitude and steadfast teachings. As she walked the stage that night, surprised by the award and Kevin's glowing speech about her, I felt so proud to witness the beautiful return on the blood, sweat, and tears of all the hard years she endured as a single mother and widow.

Bette walked through crisis and adversity with us many times in the ten years I have known her. When one of us or one of our seven children made a monumental mistake her approach to the situation was nothing short of wonder. It did not matter what the circumstances were, her response was always one of pure, untainted love. A couple years ago I was beaten and broken by a trauma that occurred with one of our children and had shut everyone out, feeling like a failure. Bette tracked me down in the grocery store parking lot, she opened my car door, took my hand, and helped me out. She wrapped her arms around me and allowed me to release it all, the pain, the fear, the anguish in a deeply tormented, disheveled display of tears and cascading mascara that surely smudged her smart overcoat. I had never experienced unconditional love in that manner. That very vulnerable moment changed my relationship with Bette, and I loved her more than I ever thought was possible from a person who was not technically my blood. Kevin and I are raising teenagers and one of the preferred activities after dinner is sitting side by side and playing with various Snap Chat filters that are designed to make you look silly, scary, or sublime. Over the years I have seen myself with perky dog ears and a long tongue, an unkempt beard, and barfing rainbows thanks to Snap Chat. My default filter from this day forward; however, will always be love because it is the filter that always makes you look and feel your best. I learned to love better and without judgement from Bette—although, if you mess with any of her grandchildren, she will kick you with a pointed boot, but that is another story.

Bette's gift of love to our family was unwavering and it was clear to me after reading Gary Chapman's "The 5 Love Languages: The Secret to Love that Lasts," her love language was "acts of service." She was the Nana who would attend all family events, big and small. Bette could be seen on the sidelines at her grandson's soccer games, in the front row of her youngest granddaughter's dance recitals, sitting in the grass at her teenage granddaughter's track meets, and the many art shows, band concerts, and graduations of her adult granddaughters. Bette walked miles hand in hand with young granddaughters on Halloween, played UNO for hours while cheeky grandchildren hit her with the "draw four" over and over, and even transported her grandson on dates before he had his license. When Kevin and I travelled to Spain for work, Bette took care of our five young children without pause. We returned to find smiling children frolicking in the yard around a new flower bed full of spring flowers, a memory and lesson she provided in our absence. Bette's perfected recipes, created with passion were treasured and often requested last minute, the most popular, her banana pudding and chocolate eclair cake. She loved to do for others and rarely said no, even when her grandkids would beg for "green marshmallow salad" twenty minutes before she planned to leave her house. Bette was always there, with warm hugs and tasty food, happy to be wherever the action was with our very large family. Bette's voice would melodiously shift, springing to the higher octave, when she saw her grandkids and spoke their names at the front door. I could hear her joyful greetings from the kitchen and the transparent contentment she found in the gift of time with her loved ones was lost on me at the time. Our home was often the definition of chaos with kids running and yelling, phones ringing, dogs barking and dog hair everywhere, but she loved it even though it was the absolute opposite of her quiet existence in Roanoke. Perhaps she loved it as she had missed out on the opportunity to play games and have fun with her kids as a single parent with so much pressure on her. Perhaps we were providing her with a "do over" with seven children she could cherish and spoil with gift of quality time and delicious food.

Bette continued to show her strength of character and abiding courage in the years I was blessed to know her. In 2016, Bette was diagnosed with breast cancer. In the five years that followed she conquered surgeries, radiation, and chemotherapy with a resolute heart and enduring faith, but the cancer kept coming back. Bette even sustained a stressful divorce in those years, having married a man not worthy of her well after her children had become adults. The divorce allowed Kevin and me to become her primary caregivers and she moved closer to us. Bette lived ten minutes from our home for almost two years and the memories I made with her in that time make my heart ache for her and the ability to make more. Bette and I worked jigsaw puzzles and ate jelly bellies in the fall with reluctant teenagers who eventually took over the activity. We planted gerbera daisies and twisted trunk hibiscus plants in her front yard in the spring with Kevin and Melinda's guidance. We rocked on her front porch enjoying an unusual sunny day in the middle of winter. We read Nicolas Sparks' *Every Breath* together in the summer, sharing a mutual love of Sunset Beach.

A couple of months ago one of Bette's sisters was ill and we sat at Bette's kitchen table drinking caramel macchiatos from Starbucks awaiting news of Joan's diagnosis. Bette had seen Joan four months earlier when all four sisters, Bette, Joan, Judy, and Debbie reconnected for an afternoon of laughs before Joan planned to move to Tennessee. Bette was struggling to process how sick Joan had become and the reality that she would not be able to see her again as her passing seemed imminent. Little did we know that Joan would remarkably recover, and we would lose our sweet Bette only a couple months later. Hoping to remind her of happier times, I asked Bette about her memories of Joan when they were living as a family near the Chesapeake Bay. Bette shared the miraculous life event of becoming an Aunt to Joan's daughter Tracy and an intimate moment of helping her younger sister bathe her newborn baby while their mother cooked an elaborate meal for the family nearby. Bette was an ever-devoted daughter, sister, aunt, mother, grandmother, and friend. When her own parents became ill, she cared for them across the miles and after they passed, she found joy tending to their gravesite flowers. Bette took care of all nine of her grandchildren any chance she got, and she loved cooking and playing games with them. Bette cared for cancer patients for decades and was a great listener to those in need. Bette volunteered for her church and with the homeless population in Roanoke most of her life. Bette is my hero and I love her endlessly.

Bette's life, like mine, had a theme of reoccurring adversity; however, through every challenge she showed up with exquisite resilience. She was our family monarch and her wisdom and ability to look past trauma and see all the good this life has to offer inspires me to be better for my own family. Bette's modest sovereignty continued to reveal itself in her final days, coupled with pure altruism. She allowed herself one moment of fragile tears with Kevin when given the news that her battle with cancer would not continue. Bette then resumed her post as our fearless protector, putting the concern for her family before her own grieving. In her final week she confessed peace in her tired eyes and acceptance in her voice, forever the devoted mother determined to safeguard her children and grandchildren from anguish.

Bette's favorite flower was the Shasta daisy, and I recently found an anonymous poem that describes Bette perfectly, I am including it below. This weekend we will plant Shasta daisies in our front yard flower bed with our five younger children, just as she did four years ago with them. Grieving is impossibility difficult but keeping Bette's memory alive by engaging in activities that brought her joy has been my first step toward healing.

Bette & Ally, 2017

Advice from a Daisy

Brighten someone's day.
Radiate beauty.
Spread cheer.
Be open.
Find room to grow.
Keep a sunny outlook.
Live with joy!

LIFE LESSON #11

Say what you need to say, carryout out
plans today as tomorrow is never promised.

On February 17, 2021 Bette was admitted to Roanoke Memorial Hospital just before midnight. Bette's very aggressive breast cancer returned for the fourth time and the lymph nodes provided deadly transport, resulting in metastasized cancer in her liver (and likely her brain). Dr. K visited her at dawn the next day and shocked us all with the news that she only had thirty days to live. Bette passed away five days later, on February 23. I was the last family member to see her that final day and as I sat with her from noon until six p.m. watching her sleep, I recall thinking about questions I wanted to ask her in the next couple of weeks.

How did you meet your husband, Dallas?
How did you know he was the one?
What is your favorite part about being a mother and grandmother?
Is there a place you wish you had visited?

I had already thanked her for the gift of her wonderful son and for treating my two children as her own and not stepchildren. I also thanked her for teaching me a more profound lesson about unconditional love on day two of her hospital stay but there was so much more I wanted to say. By day five we had packed her cards, flowers, and belongings and had planned to take her home with hospice care the following day, but Bette had another plan. Bette was awake in our final hour together; she refused her dinner but asked for a popsicle. She allowed me to feed her three bites of that Blue Bunny orange popsicle and her returned strength in each enthusiastic bite renewed my hope for more time. I waited for her to take her six p.m. medication. When Nurse Olivia left, I kissed Bette's forehead and hands and whispered, "I love you." I turned to leave, and Bette's sweet voice broke the silence between us when she told me she loved me one last time.

Bette passed away forty-four days before her 80th Birthday. We had plans for a blowout milestone birthday celebration at our favorite beach, and now she would never be able to attend it. We had plans to walk Sunset Beach to see the Kindred Spirit mailbox, a dream she had created after reading a book that still sat on her bedside table next to her Bible, more than a year after reading it. We had plans to search for shells to add to her collection in a decorative box of shells she had labelled from her trips to Jamaica with Dallas and Corolla Beach, North Carolina with her children and grandchildren. We had plans for an epic surf and turf dinner accompanied by Ruinart Champagne in a dimly lit center stage table at our favorite restaurant, Sea Blue. We had plans to sing to her while lighting a fancy cake with decades of candles to celebrate a life well lived. We had plans to create more memories as a family of fourteen and the thought of Bette not being with us has left an agonizing wound that could not be healed.

Kevin and I visited Sunset Beach days after Bette's passing to grieve. We talked to God, we walked miles and miles of sand and surf, we cried and mourned our unimaginable loss, and we attempted to process crippling heartbreak. The first day we walked west past Kindred Spirit, not having the strength to look at it, and finally paused to rest at the rock jetty that borders the canal to Calabash. I looked down in the surf, only steps from the rocks, and dancing in the mixture of sand, salt, and water was a perfect white sand dollar the size of my palm. The shell was the definition of transcendence, and I felt the presence of something greater. I believe God was holding Bette in that moment, allowing us to feel her presence. She was finally reunited with Dallas in heaven and at peace, free from cancer's raw affliction and the pain of her illness. The following week we laid Bette to rest beside her husband at a picturesque gravesite beside the Chesapeake Bay. The wind was gloriously alive that day, and I believe she was all around us, gently blowing the hair of her sisters, daughters, and granddaughters and rustling the sheet music as I attempted to sing her favorite song, "He Touched Me." Bette was no longer "shackled by a heavy burden." She had been released and as I watched the playful flurry fluctuate the abundance of funeral flowers around her urn, I smiled at the thought of her freedom. I will fiercely miss this prodigious woman of God, our profoundly selfless Nana and my deeply loving Moma every day of my life. I will forever wish I had more time. I am thankful to God for the gift of her influence to the woman I am today and the woman I hope to become because of her meritorious example.

Kindred Spirit Mailbox, Sunset Beach, NC

My final thoughts about loss and trauma, my friend? Make the time that you have left with your loved one's count. Do not take one conversation on a sports field during half time, one laugh about the family dog's daily mischief, or one internet search for the perfect shoe be taken for granted. Bette allowed me to force upon her my love of fashion, she was always such a great sport about it. One year we bought her a wonderfully soft leopard faux fur vest for her birthday, and she wore it proudly and often. She looked so stunning in that vest and it brought me so much joy to see her enjoy one of my passions. Last Christmas she complimented me on my trendy suede high-top Steve Madden sneakers and asked where I got them. It took me a week or so, but I found the shoes, in size five and ordered them for Bette as a surprise. The shoes arrived the week of her decline and as she opened the gift, three sets of eyes welled with tears knowing she would likely never wear them.

She opened the shoes six weeks after Christmas, her last Christmas. A perfect holiday where we celebrated the end of her battle with cancer and made plans for 2021, enthusiastically crafting the narrative of the start of her 8th decade. Everything changed in weeks. She had no symptoms and then she had all of them, and it was too late. We are navigating the depression that comes with devastating loss without much success. We have eaten all our feelings but feel more empty than ever. We are not sleeping and when we do, we have nightmares. The brain fog is constant and relentless. The roller coaster of emotions hits at odd times. One week following Bette's passing Kevin and I were emptying her lonely refrigerator and watering her orphaned plants. I went outside and perched on the abandoned rocking chairs remembering our last unseasonably warm afternoon on the porch two weeks ago. That night I awoke at one a.m. to a desperate panic attack, and I unleashed it all.

This was the panic attack to end all panic attacks, the worst one I have ever experienced. I fell apart and not just because of the unimaginable grief of losing Bette but twenty years of chronic adversity that was trapped behind a very dark shame shadow. Losing Bette was the straw that broke the camel's back except in this case I believe a divine intervention was in play. That early morning mystical prophesy hit me like a battering ram, the heavy timber knocking the wind from my body, and I could not catch my breath. The fury behind the action created a cataclysmic explosion of emotion. Every loud, wet, painful, guarded, vile secret or sentiment erupted from me like a raging volcano. I could not make it stop, the breakdown of my mental health took on a life of its own. My heart was racing like a prized thoroughbred at the Kentucky Derby, the thud of his heavy hoof bellowed in my ears. My eyes cascaded in violent tears, languishing over losing Bette. My voice cried out in all three octaves and my mind was flooded with every horrific memory of the cancer battle she endured, and eventually lost. Then my mind shifted to recall all the traumas, from two decades of loss, on repeat as if it were on a film reel. I saw the two opportunistic predators, their devious smiles and scandalous abuse of me burned hot on my brain. I sensed the stinging red tinge of physical suffering, ten surgeries, tumor removals, nerve damage, more abnormal cells and the ghastly effects of chemotherapy. I experienced the repeated annoying poke of my anxiety ramp up reminded of the mournful cry of ringing phones, revealing more bad news. Especially the one we received the week before at midnight, telling us Bette had passed away alone in her hospital room. Finally, I surrendered to the death grip on my heart, broken by the multifaceted layers of regret and missed opportunities. My attack was raw and merciless and just as I was about to lose all hope and give up, Kevin pulled me into his loving embrace and the attack began to subside.

Everyone grieves differently and as my journey has just begun, I cannot offer much advice here yet. What I can share, with great conviction, is say what you need to say, carryout out plans today as tomorrow is never promised. Living with regret is not an easy place to be. Take the time today to call your loved ones or better yet, visit them! Say what is on your heart. Share with them what they mean to your life. Give them a big post-COVID hug. We never know if yesterday's visit or phone conversation is our last one.

EPILOGUE

Many people have told me it is inspiring and brave to share intimate details about the chronic adversity I have experienced. While I appreciate the compliment, I feel I was called by God to do something more profound with my life experiences. It is easy to become jaded when you see how cruel life can be, but I can honestly say that being in a relationship with God gave me hope during and after the trials. The hope often came packaged with a directive to help others which is why I wrote this book. God is always giving us clues and guidance for the bountiful life he wishes us to have but we must be open to the message. At times God's memo might seem like it has typos and the instructions inconceivable for example when I was called to end my marriage. That rocky road created many obstacles but ended with my perfect life with Kevin and our beautifully blended family of seven incredible children.

I want you to harness your inner underdog and tap into the positivity that is currently hiding below the surface to find your own win. What is holding you back today from tapping into that important resource? Is it the criticism you infer from other people or the judgement you continue to inflict on yourself? What is one step you could take right now to start being more positive? 2020-2021 was a pivotal year for me regarding my reaction to what others think. My give a darn meter is officially broken because the only thing that should matter to any of us is what God thinks of us. The strain of my trauma broke me but also provided a gateway to live a fully present life full of passion, purpose, and positivity after the storms. The first step for me was putting God first and not allowing other people's harsh opinions of me tear me down any longer. The second step was addressing my shame and trauma. The healing that I have experienced by unveiling my truth in this book and jumping with confidence out of my shame shadow has changed my life. I finally love myself and am proud to see myself as a survivor and not a victim.

I mentioned in Chapter 10 that I raised my white flag and surrendered to God. The white flag is not the only piece of dramatic imagery I observed during the healing process. The trigger of a phone call with bad news in 2020 reminded me of the first phone call with bad news in 1995. I have been enduring life altering trauma for over twenty-five years, a quarter of a century. Enduring is the wrong word; I had been piling traumas on like a 13-layer cake.

Ally's 13- Layer Trauma Cake

Layer 13: Bette's death.

Layer 12: Bette's stage 4 cancer diagnosis.

Layer 11; Hysterectomy (more pre-cancerous cells.)

Layer 10: Thyroid surgery (abnormal cells.)

Layer 9: Almost losing our business. (Book 2)

Layer 8: Catastrophic financial betrayal in our business. (Book 2)

Layer 7: Mental health crisis with multiple children.

Layer 6: Three surgeries for pre-cancerous cells that kept returning.

Layer 5: Divorce.

Layer 4: Sodomized rape.

Layer 3: Incestuous sexual abuse.

Layer 2: Cancer diagnosis & chemotherapy treatment.

Layer 1: Eric was killed by a drunk driver.

The above image is what 13- layers of trauma in cake form looks like. I can share with absolute certainty that it is the most revolting cake you have ever considered tasting; you do not want to try it. The point is that my life would never have looked like this heavy cake if I had addressed each layer of trauma at their inception. Alternatively, I kept piling it on, row after row and choking it down, bite after bite, and the result, a very lopsided life. Looking at all the trauma layered up like a cake, helped me to begin the healing process of forgiveness. Beginning each day with gratitude instead of anxiety charged panic removed the margin for fear to sneak in and grind my progress to a devastating halt. That extra space in my heart, mind, and soul was fertile ground for my new passions and God's purpose to grow.

When God revealed my purpose (to help others) and new passion (writing) I was skeptical. Forgiving myself for decades of hateful inner dialogues that were fueled by Satan's lies took time, but man do I feel fierce after defeating that dragon! Not only do I feel fierce, but I am also more focused than ever. I am so proud of myself for overcoming all this heavy baggage that remained after trauma and with fresh eyes and my burden lifted, I am excited to help all of you! When you awake with fresh eyes after trauma has rendered you deaf, dumb, and blind you must do a careful assessment. My assessment indicated that I needed to make some changes to create a strong foundation for my mental health so here is what I did.

I stopped wearing yoga pants and the messy bun every single day. I started doing my hair and make-up each day and wearing a confidence producing outfit several days a week that made me feel good about myself. I started scheduling meetings outside the house. The year of online Zoom meetings allowed me to become lazy about my appearance which fueled my depression even more. By taking the time to put cute outfits together, I was tapping back into my first passion, fashion, and it put a sassy pep back in my step to put more effort into my daily appearance!

When you experience trauma, you often lose sight of the person you were before the trauma occurred. This definitely happened to me but was amplified by the image that stared back at me in the mirror. I did not look like myself at all. I had begun to lose my vibrant red hair; it was browning out as I turned forty. I did not care at first, distracted by excessive depression. But once I woke up and my purpose was clear, I wanted to feel more like the old confident me before trauma, so I discovered a wonderful color treatment technique called balyage. It allows me to return to my original hue more naturally and with less maintenance. The other thing I noticed, over ten years I had gained about fifty pounds...maybe more. I am going to be real with you once again, my friend, I have attempted to lose the weight and failed at least twenty-five times...maybe more. Excuses were easy and creative. Allow me to share my long list of excuses which drove my goal to lose the weight over the years to a grinding halt.

Ally's Excuses...

I twisted my ankle and cannot exercise.

I hurt my back and cannot exercise.

I overslept and cannot exercise.

Going to dinner is much more fun than doing exercise.

Drinking wine is much more fun than doing exercise.

Doing just about anything is more fun than doing exercise.

There is a lonely bottle of wine on the counter, and I need to drink the last couple of glasses before it goes bad.

There is no food in the house, time to order pizza...again.

The kids are eating ice cream, one scoop will not hurt me.

A friend or business colleague came to visit, and we had to wine and dine them...again.

Depression dominated my behavior after someone stole from us...again.

Depression dominated my behavior after someone sued us...again.

Depression dominated my behavior after someone was diagnosed with cancer...again.

Depression dominated my behavior after she lost her battle with cancer and passed away.

If I look unattractive and overweight, I will be safe from predators and future attacks.

I just shared every excuse that was readily available in my memory from the last few years of triggers that had me enthusiastically swan diving off the wagon back into overindulgence of wine and emotional eating. My swan dives were also prompted by many alluring reasons to celebrate from a very blessed, happy marriage. But fifty-plus pounds is serious, and ten years is ridiculous...enough is enough. I am embarrassed that it took me ten years to take action and to be successful, but I am excited to tell you that I finally figured it out. For me it took setting the big goal (losing fifty pounds) and not allowing any celebrations of smaller goals to derail me. In the past I would celebrate with wine or a treat after I lost ten pounds; that celebration inevitably continued for weeks (or months) and eventually I gained the ten pounds back and was forced to return to square one. I also had to develop a slightly different mindset about food. When I left my first husband, I was at my goal weight. I was doing a lot of walking and soul searching about leaving and was not eating very much. At that time, I thought of food only as a fuel, not a treat. I was more focused on providing a safe, happy life for my children and celebrating was the furthest thing from my mind. I am delighted and thankful to be living a life that provides regular reasons to celebrate but if I end up dying an early death from obesity, all will be lost. Ladies, it is also much more difficult to lose weight as a woman and my journey, even more challenging. I am only working with half of my thyroid and my hormones are less normal than other women my age. But I am not going to add that to my list of past excuses. The other thing that made losing weight hard: I would constantly compare myself to my husband. Kevin can lose weight twice as fast as I can, and he was always ready to celebrate way before I would be able to on my current course. That is life, ladies, but we do not have to allow comparisons and the unique makeup of male genes to make us feel hopeless. We simply need to do our research and figure out a plan that works for us. I think I have found it! I am excited to share my plan and my journey in my second book so stay tuned!

I started using my voice. Remember what I said earlier, going through the motions in this gift called life is operating as a victim, but making intentional decisions is living as a fierce survivor. I will always battle the tendency to be a people pleaser above my own personal wellbeing but my desire to live as a fierce survivor is going to win that battle going forward. We all have those people in our lives that attempt to overpower us with their own agendas, attempting to treat us as their victims. Their selfish venture can transpire as a large-scale violation or a seemingly small interaction, but it does not really matter because it is a pattern they have adopted. But that does not mean; however, that you must allow them to treat you as their minion. I had to start putting my money where my mouth was and here is the thing, you do not have to be rude about it. I was at a meeting recently where a much older man attempted to bully me into switching seats with him, exerting himself between myself and my husband. Friends, I do not sit beside anyone but my husband at events and this man's presumptuous demand of me lit my redheaded, Scorpio short temper on fire. But losing my temper would only show that I was not in control of the situation so here is what I did. I smiled confidently and made a joke out of him not wanting to sit near me and he returned to his original seat. It seems like a silly example but why do we allow people to bulldoze us without our consent for their own selfish reasons? Put your foot down and you can absolutely be a lady (or gentleman) while doing it.

I had to find my smile again. When you live in a perpetual state of depression after trauma is triggered your face forgets what your default expression should be. Sadly, mine was typically not a smile. Behind my eyes I was battling crippling anxiety and I had forgotten how to smile. My method for finding it has been smiling and greeting every stranger I encounter on the street. I had to reprogram my body to hold my smile as the default. My smile is still not as organic as I wish it were, but I am a work in progress for sure! Finding my smile was the final piece of my goal to become more authentic. I mentioned earlier about the "industrial smile" which I learned about from a Vietnamese friend, Dan. Basically you place a chop stick in between your two rows of teeth to create the most natural, yet glamorous smile. Dan and my dear friend, Charmaine, helped me get ready for the book photo shoot and I am lucky to have such wise beauty advisors, and am most thankful to also call them friends.

I am so excited that you chose to walk this journey with me, and I have one more resource for you! I am including a study guide for further discussion. The study guide will allow you to walk through healing your own traumas with important questions you can talk about with your own Bible study tribe, family, or book club. I want to continue to support you so follow me on Instagram @fiercetigerlady for daily inspiration! Or @stayfiercetigerlady on TikTok. I look forward to meeting you and to growing more fantastically fierce together!

I shared in Chapter 10 that part of my plan to actively take my power back during adversity involved making plans. I also told you about my commitment to health in Chapter 10 and this Epilogue. In my next book I will give you the gift of wisdom from this current journey toward abundant health once I officially have lost the fifty pounds. I have big plans once I reach that goal and those plans are vulnerable, raw, and beautifully authentic. Until next time my friend, #stayfierce and bask in the afterglow of all the thrilling experiences that harvest your positivity, passion, and purpose.

The End

The Gift of Scripture

I pray that the lessons I shared with you allow you to find peace with the struggles you are currently navigating. As I wish you well and say goodbye (for now) allow me to share some of God's promises to begin the journey through your current storm. He will rescue you out of the harbor of misery and transport you to sanctuary if you let him. I believe our lives can change in a moment; it is all about where you put your focus. God bless you and keep you now and forever, my courageous friend.

1 Peter 5:10
And the God of all grace, who called you
to his eternal glory in Christ, after you
have suffered a little while, will himself re-
store you and make you strong, firm, and
steadfast.

Joshua 1:9-10
Have I not commanded you? Be strong and
courageous. Do not be afraid; do not be
discouraged, for the Lord your God will be
with you wherever you go.

Philippians 4:6-7
Do not be anxious about anything, but in
every situation, by prayer and petition, with
thanksgiving, present your requests to God.
And the peace of God, which transcends all
understanding, will guard your hearts and
your minds in Christ Jesus.

The Gift of Music

I mentioned several times that music has always been my one of my first passions, and it continues to drive me forward with positivity each day of my life. I create playlists a lot based on the season of life I am in, they bring me back to a place, a lesson, or profound wisdom. I am including a #fiercetigerlady playlist for you below.

#FIERCETIGERLADY: A PLAYLIST

"Afterglow" by Ed Sheeran
"A Thousand Years" by Christina Perry
"Water Runs Dry" by Boyz II Men
"Come Undone" by Duran Duran
"Love Me Back to Life" by Celine Dion
"When We Dance" by Sting
"The Sun is Rising" by Britt Nicole
"Wouldn't it Be Nice" by The Beach Boys
"To Cry About" by Mary Margaret O'Hara
"Still Standing" by Elton John
"Underdog" by Alicia Keys
"Sister" by K. Flay
"The Champion" (featuring Ludacris) by Carrie Underwood
"Ok Not to Be Ok" by Demi Lovato and Marshmello
"Jekyll & Hyde" by Plumb
"Everything" by Lauren Daigle
"Slow Burn" by Kacey Musgraves
"Redhead" (featuring Reba McEntire) by Caylee Hammock
"Ode to My Family" by The Cranberries
"Smooth Criminal" by Michael Jackson
"Run the World (Girls)" by Beyoncé
"Rewrite the Stars" by Zac Efron and Zendaya
"Bird Set Free" by Sia
"Shallow" by Lady Gaga and Bradly Cooper
"Eye of the Tiger" by Survivor

STUDY QUESTIONS
(Group Discussion)

Meeting #1

In the intro I shared that my process of overcoming trauma began with adopting the hashtag #stayfierce which was an important reminder to see myself as a survivor and no longer a victim. Which hashtag represents you as you begin your journey?

#_____

Discuss your morning routine as a group. What is working? What has you frustrated? What is a commitment you could make today to begin crafting a new routine that would allow for ultimate success?

_____
_____
_____
_____
_____
_____
_____
_____

What do you do (or could you do) when you wake up with no motivation, or when you are feeling defeated? How do you conquer the anxiety monster who is trying to drag you back to your depressive state and stifle your progression toward your current goals? _____

_____
_____
_____
_____
_____
_____
_____
_____

What does your inner dialogue sound like? Is it one of self-love or self-deprivation? Who or what is affecting how you see yourself? How could you re-write that script?

_____
_____
_____
_____
_____
_____
_____
_____

How do you walk through loss? What does your support system look like? Who are you talking to? If you are not talking about it, which person in your life could be your sounding board? Have you considered joining a support group or finding a counselor? _____

_____
_____
_____
_____
_____
_____
_____

What are you grateful for today? Make a list of five things...

(1)_____

(2)_____

(3)_____

(4)_____

(5)_____

What are five things you want to talk to God about today (prayer list, goals, setbacks)?

(1)_____

(2)_____

(3)_____

(4)_____

(5)_____

STUDY QUESTIONS
(Group Discussion)

Meeting #2

What is holding you back from being a positive person? What changes could you make to allow yourself to wake up each day with optimism and hope? _____

_____

_____

_____

_____

_____

_____

_____

What do you feel shameful about in your life/past? What would it feel like to finally release the burden of that secret?

_____

_____

_____

_____

_____

_____

Are you holding on to regret about your mistakes or sins made in the past? What would it feel like to ask God for forgiveness? What would it feel like to be free of those thoughts by forgiving yourself and moving on?

_____

_____

_____

_____

_____

_____

Write down five things you love about yourself.

(1)_____

(2)_____

(3)_____

(4)_____

(5)_____

Write down five ways your spouse/significant other/friends make you feel loved and supported. If it is difficult to answer this question, what do you believe to be the solution?

(1)_____

(2)_____

(3)_____

(4)_____

(5)_____

If there is a strain in your relationship with your spouse/significant other and what is the source of it? How could you begin the conversation that would ultimately repair your relationship? Do you need to enlist the help of a counselor?

_____
_____
_____
_____
_____
_____
_____
_____

STUDY QUESTIONS
(Group Discussion)

Meeting #3

How are you spending your time in solitude? What activities (or passions) could you add to your routine that would bless you personally and/or professionally? _____

_____

_____

_____

_____

_____

_____

_____

_____

Jim Rohn tells us, "We are the average of the five people we spend the most time with." Who are your five people and what are their roles in your life? (family, work, personal)

_____

_____

_____

_____

_____

_____

_____

_____

_____

What is your intuition telling you about your five people?
Do any of them need to be re-purposed to a less influential
role in your life?

(1)_____

(2)_____

(3)_____

(4)_____

(5)_____

What is your biggest fear? Which impactful Bible verse or
favorite inspirational quote could you memorize and use as
a mantra to get you out of that panicked frame of mind?

_____
_____
_____
_____
_____
_____
_____
_____
_____

What big decision is looming in your life right now? How
could you craft a prayer to allow God to weigh in? How
could you be more open to his wisdom in your daily life?__

_____
_____
_____
_____
_____
_____
_____
_____

If you are being led to step outside of your comfort zone in work or home life, how could you craft a plan that allows you to take baby steps toward a bigger goal each week? __

_____

_____

_____

_____

_____

_____

_____

_____

_____

_____

STUDY QUESTIONS
(Group Discussion)

Meeting #4

How are you feeling about your calendar? Do you need to set better boundaries? What is one boundary you could set today to remove some stress from your life? _____

_____

_____

_____

_____

_____

_____

_____

_____

Are you being fully present for the people in your life? What is one change you could make that would allow you to be more available to your spouse, children, or friends?

_____

_____

_____

_____

_____

_____

_____

_____

What is your current career or primary role in life? What are two - four aspects of the position that you are passionate about? If this is a difficult question, what could you do to discover passions in your current role?

_____
_____
_____
_____
_____
_____
_____
_____
_____

What are the pros and cons of your current role? Which list has more?

Pros_____
_____
_____
_____
_____
_____
_____
_____
_____

Cons_____
_____
_____
_____
_____
_____
_____

If you are unhappy in your current role, what could you do today to attempt to fix it or to begin to look for another opportunity? How would you begin the conversation?

_____
_____
_____
_____
_____
_____
_____
_____
_____
_____
_____
_____
_____
_____
_____
_____
_____
_____

STUDY QUESTIONS
(Group Discussion)

Meeting #5

What are two of your personal passions? What would it look like and feel like to be able to do one or both of your passions once a month or more frequently?

_____

_____

_____

_____

_____

_____

_____

_____

_____

Did you take the Enneagram or Myers-Briggs's personality test? If so, what is your personality type? How is that information leading you in your discovery of new passions and your ultimate happiness personally and professionally? ____

_____

_____

_____

_____

_____

_____

_____

_____

_____

What did the Covid-19 Quarantine teach you? How did you handle being confined to your home for over a year? What is the first thing you did when you felt safe going back out?_____

_____

_____

_____

_____

_____

_____

_____

_____

Who did you miss the most during the Quarantine? Which relationships need a tune up? What is it you want to say to your loved ones that you have not yet said? When could you make time to say it? _____

_____

_____

_____

_____

_____

_____

_____

_____

If you have lost a loved one recently, what do you wish you could say to them? What activity could you do to honor their memory? _____

_____

_____

_____

_____

_____

_____

_____

STUDY QUESTIONS
(Group Discussion)

Meeting #6

Which trauma from your past continues to haunt you every single day? What would forgiveness look like? If you forgave yourself and removed blame, could you find freedom from the nightmare? _____

_____
_____
_____
_____
_____
_____
_____
_____

How are you going to #stayfierce from this day forward? What would it look and feel like to move from victim to survivor? Was your meeting 1 hashtag a good fit or do you need to adjust it?

_____
_____
_____
_____
_____
_____
_____
_____
_____
_____
_____
_____
_____
_____

Final Hashtag: #_____
Fear Mantra: _____

Goals:

(1)_____
_____
_____
_____

(2)_____
_____
_____
_____

(3)_____
_____
_____
_____

(4)_____
_____
_____
_____

(5)_____
_____
_____
_____

ACKNOWLEDGEMENTS

Michael Vest Photography
Fifty Love Photograpy
Amodeo Photography

Jordan Smith
Thank you for permission to include your father's poem.

CPSIA information can be obtained
at www.ICGtesting.com
Printed in the USA
BVHW011141070322
630817BV00002B/56